CUDDLY KNITTED ANIMALS

Publication data

First published in Great Britain 2014 by Search Press Limited, Wellwood, North Farm Road, Tunbridge Wells, Kent TN2 3DR

World rights reserved by Christophorus Verlag GmbH, Freiburg/Germany

Originally published in Germany as *Tierische Freunde* by Christophorus Verlag GmbH & Co., Freiburg, 2012

English translation by Sharon Earle for Cicero Translations

English edition produced by GreenGate Publishing Services, Tonbridge

Concept, designs and production: Caprice Birker
Photography: Robert Birker
Styling: Caprice Birker
Editing and technical drawings: Arnhilt Tittes
Layout and jacket design: GrafikwerkFreiburg

ISBN: 978-1-84448-925-1

Printed in China

CUDDLY KNITTED ANIMALS

Caprice Birker

SEARCH PRESS

DEAR READER

My great enthusiasm for knitting – and hoarding yarn – has led to a slight addiction to wool. I seem to develop 'friendships' with my favourite yarns and I'm quite sure I'm not the only one!

Not long ago, I came across a beautiful, soft, brown yarn and suddenly a cuddly mouse was sitting on my desk, with one leg longer than the other and one ear bigger than the other. Despite being just a prototype, I felt he had already become a true friend!

While working on this first design, I realised that there were many more friends to be found in my store of yarns. And so, one after another, the first animals were created. It was not long before these endearing characters had found new friends in my own family and among my circle of friends.

I would like to give a special thanks to my two daughters, who encouraged me with lots of exclamations of "How sweet!" as well as with useful tips and helping me to name the animals. Making these cuddly friends was a great experience for me and I would be really pleased if my friends were to become your friends too!

While all these projects are made from the same basic design, you will be amazed at how easily each animal develops its own individual character.

I wish you lots of fun with your knitting.

Regards,

4

CONTENTS

BEFORE YOU BEGIN

Before reaching for needles and yarn and starting to knit your first cuddly friend, please take the time to read the following information. It contains general tips and explanations that are essential for understanding the instructions and for making each animal.

Following the knitting instructions

The animals are mostly knitted in the round using a set of double-pointed needles, although there are some exceptions, such as the hare's ears and the dragon's wings. Often, when knitting in the round, the stitches on each needle are worked in the same way, in which case the chart shows only the stitches on the first needle and these should be repeated on the other three needles. However, sometimes the way the animal is constructed means that the stitches only need to be repeated twice or not at all. Details are provided with the specific knitting patterns. For most of the faces, all the stitches to be knitted are given in the chart.

Finishing off

Yarns should always be finished off just before decreasing or stuffing. Often, it is enough to pull the yarn to the inside through the wadding.

Stuffing the animals

The animals are all stuffed with wadding. It is easiest if you stuff the body parts before the opening gets small, so as soon as you start decreasing, you should keep this in mind, especially when it comes to small parts such as the hands and feet. This is described in the general instructions but is not always mentioned in the individual instructions for the animals.

When it comes to stuffing, follow these guidelines:

- Stuff legs and arms before the opening gets too small.
- For very thin arms and legs, use the blunt end of a pencil or a rounded knitting needle to push in the wadding.
- Do not stuff the tops of the limbs because these flat areas act as joints.
- Not all the tails are stuffed. Refer to the individual instructions.
- Stuff the body and head just before completing the head.
- Do not stuff the ears.

Yarns and needles

The animals are knitted in sock yarn or similar fine, strong yarn, using a set of 2.25mm or 2.5mm (UK size 13 or 12/US size 1 or 2) double-pointed needles. You can use other yarn types and the appropriate needles but the sizing will be different. You can also use other yarns for different effects – see Uni the Unicorn and Donald the Dragon (page 98) who are knitted with different yarns and 3.0mm (UK size 11/US size 3) needles and therefore come out larger than the other animals.

Keeping track

It is useful to have a row or round counter so you do not lose track of your progress. Alternatively, you can photocopy the instructions and tick off each round or row as you complete it.

Understanding the knitting instructions

Sometimes the stitch distribution on the needles is given to help you. This should be read from the 1st to the 4th needle.

Example:

9/12/9/10 means you should put 9 stitches on needle 1, 12 stitches on needle 2, 9 stitches on needle 3 and 10 stitches on needle 4. The charts show the needles reading from right to left.

At the end of a round, in which stitches are increased or decreased, the distribution of stitches is sometimes included, as well as the total number of stitches you should have. This is useful as a guide to where you are when knitting and it is helpful if the same number of stitches are not increased or decreased on all needles.

Example:

3rd round: K25, * k1, k2tog *, repeat from * to * five more times, k13 [13/12/13/12; 50 sts]. This means knit 25 stitches, * knit 1, knit two stitches together *, repeat from * to * another five times, knit 13 stitches for a total of 50 stitches arranged with 13 stitches on the first needles, 12 on the second and so on.

Occasionally the stitches to be knitted may be given with a plus sign (+). This acts as a guide, indicating the needle to which an instruction refers.

Example:
K5, k2tog, k3, k2tog, knit 5 + 5 stitches [5/5/5/5; 20 sts].
This means: on needle 1 you should knit 5 stitches; on needle 2 you should knit 2 stitches together, knit 3 stitches, knit 2 stitches together; on needle 3 knit 5 stitches and on needle 4 knit 5 stitches.

Knitting short rounds or rows

In some cases a number of stitches in a round are worked for an extra two rows at a time to add shaping, as on the dog's tail and the hare's face. When stitches are knitted back and forth in short rows or rounds in this way it is important to loop the yarn around the next stitch (which will not be knitted), to avoid creating a hole. This does not apply for the short rows of the heel turn when knitting the back of the head.

Example:
K6, turn the work and purl back over the 6 sts, turn the work and knit back over the 6 sts, k5.
This means: knit 6 stitches, loop the yarn around the next stitch, turn work, purl 6 stitches, loop the yarn around the next stitch, turn work, knit 6 stitches, knit 5 stitches.

General

Unless otherwise stated, the animals are all knitted using stocking stitch (knit on right-side rows, purl on wrong-side rows).

Making increases

Increase a stitch (inc1) by inserting the left needle from front to back into the horizontal bar of yarn between the two stitches.

SYMBOLS AND ABBREVIATIONS

- □ = K1 (knit 1 stitch)
- ⊟ = P1 (purl 1 stitch)
- ☑ = K2tog (knit 2 stitches together)
- ☑ = K3tog (knit 3 stitches together)
- ☒ = P2tog (purl 2 stitches together)
- ☒ = P3tog (purl 3 stitches together)
- ⑤ = Inc1 (increase one stitch knitwise by picking up the bar between stitches)
- ② = Inc1 (increase one stitch purlwise)

- ⊣ = Kfb (knit into the front then back of the same stitch to double the stitches)
- ▦ = K2 (see the written instructions in each case)
- ▦ = K1, p1 (see the written instructions in each case)
- ☰ = P 1 row over these sts, turn and k 1 row, turn and p 1 row
- RB = Beginning of round
- ● = Pick up 1 stitch from the knitted item
- ■ = Stitch on a stitch holder
- ▦ = Leave 1 stitch on the needle or stitch holder in short rows or rounds

THE BASIC DESIGN

Each cuddly animal is knitted in one piece using the same basic pattern but with specific variations. The knitting sequence is the same for all the animals, starting with the torso and then the back of the head, each leg and foot and each arm and hand. Some of the faces have a forehead and nose, while others have a one-stage face. Most animals have a special face and instructions are given in each case. Individual instructions are also given for the ears and tail.

Basic construction sequence:

1. Knit the torso and back of the head in one piece. The stitches for joining the arms, legs and tail are always the same and are created on the torso and left on stitch holders ready for use. These stitches should be transferred to the knitting needles and worked as instructed for each animal.
2. Knit the lower limbs.
3. Knit the upper limbs.
4. Knit the tail.
5. Knit the face. Embroider the facial details as instructed.
6. Knit the ears.

It is important to keep to the sequence because it is more difficult to knit the arms, legs and tail on to a stuffed body.

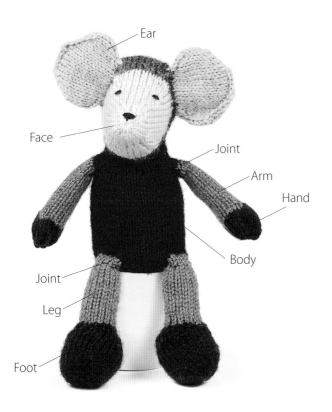

Knitting the Torso

Materials

- Yarn as listed for each animal
- Set of 5 double-pointed knitting needles in the size specified in the pattern
- 10 stitch holders (you can use a smooth contrasting yarn threaded through the stitches and knotted in a ring to stop the stitches falling off)

The start of every animal is at the centre back. Work in rounds of stocking stitch.

Cast on 2 stitches four times on the set of needles. (These instructions are charted on page 12.)

Round 1: Join into a round, making sure the stitches are not twisted, and knit [8 sts].

Round 2: * K1, inc1, k1 *, repeat from * to * three more times. (Inc1 by picking up the bar before the next stitch and knitting it) [12 sts].

Round 3: Knit to the end.

Round 4: * K1, inc1, k1, inc1, k1 *, repeat from * to * three more times [20 sts].

Round 5: Knit to the end.

Round 6: * K1, inc1, k3, inc1, k1 *, repeat from * to * three more times [28 sts].

Round 7: Knit to the end.

Round 8: * K1, inc1, k5, inc1, k1 *, repeat from * to * three more times [36 sts].

Round 9: Knit to the end.

Round 10: * K1, inc1, k7, inc1, k1 *, repeat from * to * three more times [44 sts].

Round 11: Knit to the end.

Round 12:

Needle 1: K1, inc1, k9, inc1, k1.

Needle 2: K1, inc1, k10.

Needle 3: Work as for needle 1.

Needle 4: K10, inc1, k1.

Distribution of stitches: 13/12/13/12 [50 sts].

Rounds 13–14: Knit.

On rounds 15 and 18, the stitches for the tail are created on the first needle and the stitches for the legs are created on the other three needles.

Round 15:

Needle 1: K4, kfb five times, k4 [18 sts].

Needle 2: K10, kfb twice [14 sts].

Needle 3: Kfb four times, k5, kfb four times [21 sts].

Needle 4: Kfb twice, k10 [14 sts].

Distribution of stitches: 18/14/21/14 [67 sts].

Round 16: Knit the round as tightly as possible.

Now transfer the stitches you created in the last round for the legs on to two stitch holders and the stitches for the tail on to another stitch holder as follows:

Needle 1: Lift 4 stitches on to a new knitting needle, * place 1 stitch on a stitch holder, lift 1 stitch over on to the knitting needle *, repeat from * to * four more times. Close the stitch holder and then lift the remaining 4 stitches from needle 1 over on to the new knitting needle with the other 4 stitches.

Needle 2: Lift 10 stitches over on to a new knitting needle, place 1 stitch on a second stitch holder, lift 1 stitch on to the knitting needle, place 1 stitch on stitch holder, lift 1 stitch over on to the knitting needle.

Needle 3: * Place 1 stitch on the same stitch holder (which has 2 stitches on it so far), lift 1 stitch over on to a knitting needle *, repeat from * to * three more times, close the second stitch holder, then lift 5 stitches over on to the knitting needle, ** place 1 stitch on a third stitch holder, lift 1 stitch over on to the knitting needle **, repeat from ** to ** three more times.

Needle 4: Place 1 stitch on the same stitch holder (which has 4 stitches on it so far), lift 1 stitch over on to a new knitting needle, place 1 stitch on the stitch holder, lift 1 stitch over on to the knitting needle, close the third stitch holder, lift 10 stitches over on to the knitting needle.

Distribution of stitches: 13/12/13/12 [50 sts]. On the stitch holder for the tail you should have 5 stitches and on each stitch holder for the legs you should have 6 stitches.

Round 17: Knit as tightly as possible.

Round 18: Work as for round 15.

Round 19: In this round, the first of each of the doubled stitches that will later be left on stitch holders should be purled. This is so that these stitches fit into the form of the stocking-stitched body. Work as follows:

Needle 1: K4, * p1, k1 *, repeat from * to * four more times, k4.

Needle 2: K10, p1, k1, p1, k1.

Needle 3: * P1, k1 *, repeat from * to * another three times, k5, ** p1, k1 **, repeat from ** to ** another three times.

Needle 4: P1, k1, p1, k1 then k10.

Transfer the purled stitches on to three stitch holders in the same way as for round 16.

Distribution of stitches: 13/12/13/12 [50 sts]. In this round you should have placed 5 stitches on a tail-stitch holder and 6 stitches on each of two leg-stitch holders.

Round 20: Knit as tightly as possible.

Rounds 21–32: Knit.

Round 33:

Needle 1: K1, k2tog, k7, k2tog, k1.

Needle 2: K1, k2tog, k9.

Needle 3: Work as for the needle 1.

Needle 4: K9, k2tog, k1.

Distribution of stitches: 11/11/11/11 [44 sts].

Rounds 34–35: Knit.

On rounds 36 and 39, the stitches for the arms are created on needles 2 and 4.

Round 36:

Needles 1 + 3: K1, k2tog, k5, k2tog, k1.

Needles 2 + 4: K1, k2tog, kfb 5 times, k2tog, k1.

Distribution of stitches: 9/14/9/14 [46 sts].

Round 37: Knit as tightly as possible.

Transfer the stitches for the arms on to two stitch holders, in the same way as the legs as follows:

Needles 2 + 4: Lift 2 stitches over on to a new knitting needle, * place 1 stitch on the stitch holder, lift 1 stitch over on to the knitting needle *, repeat from * to * four more times, close the stitch holder, lift 2 stitches over on to the knitting needle.

Distribution of stitches: 9/9/9/9 [36 sts]. In this round you should have placed 5 stitches for each arm on to a stitch holder (one holder for each arm).

Round 38: Knit.

Round 39:

Needles 1 + 3: K1, k2tog, k3, k2tog, k1.

Needles 2 + 4: K2tog, kfb 5 times, k2tog.

Distribution of stitches: 7/12/7/12 [38 sts].

Round 40:

Needles 1 + 3: Knit tightly.

Needles 2 + 4: K1, * p1, k1 *, repeat from * to * four more times, k1.
Transfer the purled stitches on to two stitch holders, proceeding
in the same way as for round 37.

Distribution of stitches: 7/7/7/7 [28 sts]. In this round you should
have placed 5 more stitches for each arm on to stitch holders.

Round 41: Knit as tightly as possible.

Round 42: Knit.

Round 43: * K1, k2tog, k1, k2tog, k1 *, repeat from * to * on the
other three needles [5/5/5/5 = 20 sts].

Rounds 44–47: Knit.

You have now knitted the torso and neck.

Torso chart

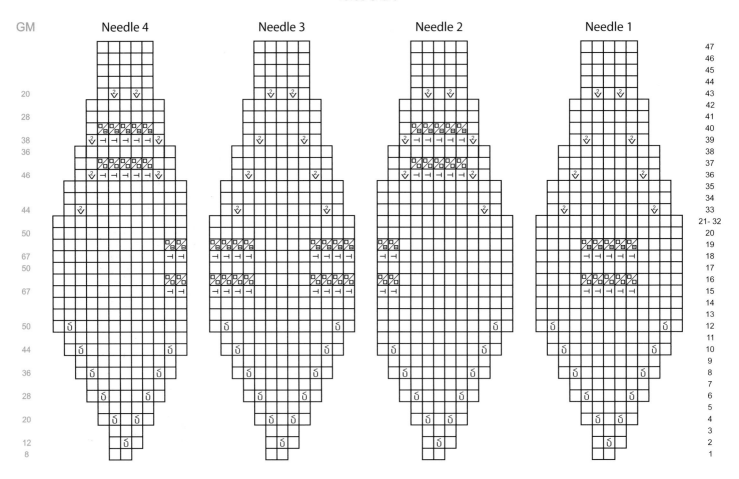

This chart shows the pattern for the torso. The stitches on each
needle are knitted differently. Refer to the written instructions for
information on transferring the stitches for the limbs and tail on to
stitch holders.

Knitting the Back of the Head

Knit the back of the head directly after round 47 of the body. You should have 5 stitches on each of the four needles to start. You will need two more stitch holders.

Round 1: * k1, inc1 *, repeat from * to * three more times, k1. Repeat round 1 on each needle [9/9/9/9; 36 sts].

Round 2: Knit all stitches.

Round 3: K31, leaving the final 5 stitches unworked. Now redistribute the stitches as follows:

Move the 5 unworked stitches from needle 4 on to needle 1 and then move the first 5 stitches of needle 2 on to needle 1 as well. Needle 1 now has 19 stitches.

Put all the remaining stitches (4 from needle 2, 9 from needle 3 and 4 from needle 4) on to a stitch holder, maintaining that order [17 sts].

The back of the head is made like a heel turn on a sock.

Starting with the stitch that was the 5th stitch of needle 4, work the 19 stitches on the needle in rows of stocking stitch.

Row 4: Knit all stitches [19 sts].

Row 5: Purl.

Rows 6–19: Work in stocking stitch (repeat rows 4 and 5). From here, the actual heel turn starts.

Row 20: K4, k2tog, k7, k2tog. Turn work.

Row 21: Slip 1, p7, p2tog. Turn work.

Row 22: Slip 1, k7, k2tog. Turn work.

Rows 23–28: Continue working in the same way until only the original 9 stitches on the first needle are left. Cut off the yarn and fasten off. The start of the round for the face (next) is the 1st stitch of this needle when knitting from right to left. Leave these stitches on a stitch holder until needed.

Chart for the back of the head

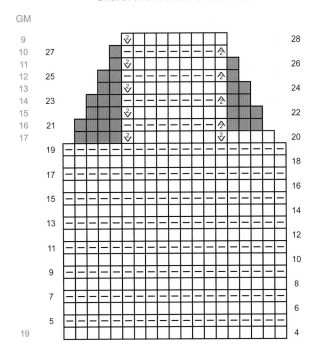

This chart shows the pattern for the back of the head, starting at row 4, after the stitches have been redistributed.

Knitting the Legs

Materials

- Yarn as listed for your chosen animal
- Set of 5 double-pointed knitting needles in the size specified in the pattern
- Wadding

It is best to knit the legs to the body before stuffing the body. The length of the legs can be varied. Fifteen rounds correspond to about 3cm (1¼in); twenty rounds correspond to about 4cm (1½in). Some animals, such as the mole (page 52), have shorter legs, while others, such as the monkey (page 36), need longer ones.

Each leg is worked from the top down, starting at the right and working from the very beginning of the knitting. The yellow dots in the photo below show the start point for each leg. It is important to take account of this, as the knitting instructions for the various different feet refer to this start of round.

Work in rounds of stocking stitch.

Lift the two sets of 6 stitches left for each leg from the stitch holders and distribute equally on to a set of four needles.

Round 1–4: Join into a round and knit four rounds [12 sts]. These four rounds form the joint and should not be stuffed with wadding.

Round 5: * K1, inc1, k4, inc1, k1 *, repeat from * to * once more [16 sts].

Round 6 onwards: Knit in rounds until the desired length is reached. Pull the starting yarn slightly before finishing off, so that the stitches of the joining rows pull together a bit, making the stitches look nicer.

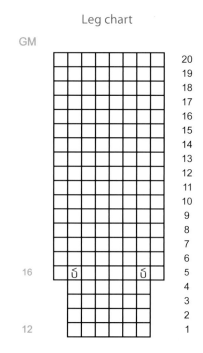

Leg chart

This chart shows half the stitches for the leg. Repeat the stitches once on each round.

The yellow dots mark the starting point for each leg.

Knitting the Feet

For each foot, just continue knitting on after each leg. There are two different feet for the animals in this book: standard feet and hooves. Follow the instructions for the type of foot required.

Standard feet

Round 1: K4, inc1, k8, inc1, k4 [4/5/4/5; 18 sts].

Round 2: Knit.

Round 3: K15, transfer the last 3 stitches to a stitch holder. Redistribute the remaining stitches over three needles as follows: Put the last 3 stitches on to needle 1 with the first 2 stitches of needle 1. Arrange the next 5 stitches on needle 2. Put the next 5 stitches on needle 3.

Distribution of stitches: 5/5/5/(+ 3 on stitch holder) [18 sts].

Work in stocking stitch.

Row 4: * K1, inc1 *, repeat from * to * three more times, k1. Repeat on needles 2 and 3 [27 sts + 3 left on needle]. Turn work.

Row 5: Slip 1, p26. Turn work.

Row 6: K9. To shape the feet, k9, turn and p9, turn and k9, looping the yarn around the next stitch each time before you turn to prevent a hole forming. K6 then loop the yarn around the next stitch to avoid a hole. Turn work.

Row 7: P21 then loop the yarn around the next stitch. Turn work.

Row 8: K6 then k9, turn and p9, turn and k9, looping the yarn around as before. K9 plus the 3 stitches that you put on the stitch holder in round 3 [30sts]. Close up the work in a round again.

Round 9: K3tog, k21, k3tog, k3 stitches [26 sts].

Rounds 10–16: Knit all stitches.

Stuff the leg with wadding, avoiding the joint area.

Stuff the foot with wadding.

Round 17: K2tog thirteen times [13 sts].

Round 18: Knit.

Before pulling together, stuff with some extra wadding, if necessary. Cut off the yarn, pull through the remaining stitches and fasten off. The right and left foot are knitted in the same way.

Standard foot chart

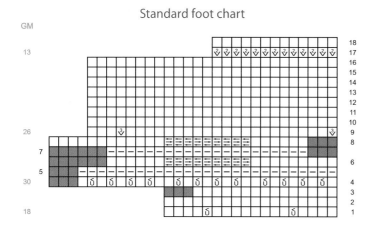

This chart shows the pattern for the standard foot. Stitches shaded purple are not knitted.

Hoof

Work directly from the 16 stitches of the leg.

Round 1: * K1, inc1 *, repeat from * to * six more times, k1. Repeat once more from the beginning [30 sts].

Rounds 2–3: Knit all stitches.

Round 4: K1, inc1, k28, inc1, k1 [32 sts].

Rounds 5–8: Knit.

Round 9: Purl.

Stuff the leg with wadding, avoiding the joint area.

Round 10: K2tog sixteen times [16 sts].

Stuff the foot with wadding.

Rounds 11–14: Knit.

Round 15: K2tog eight times [8 sts].

Before pulling together, stuff with some extra wadding, if necessary. Cut off the yarn, pull through the remaining stitches and fasten off. The right and left hoof are knitted in the same way.

Standard hoof chart

This chart shows half the stitches for the hoof. Continue each round on the second pair of needles, working the chart in mirror image.

Knitting the Arms

Materials

- Yarn as listed for your chosen animal
- Set of 5 double-pointed knitting needles in the size specified in the pattern
- Wadding

It is best to knit the arms on to the body before it has been stuffed. The length of the arms can be varied depending on the animal you are making. Fifteen rounds correspond to about 3cm (1¼in). Twenty rounds correspond to about 4cm (1½in). Some animals, such as the mole (page 52), have shorter arms while others, such as the monkey (page 36), have longer ones. The right arm is begun under the armpit front right (see the photograph below left) while the left arm is begun at the shoulder front right (see the photograph below right). The yellow dot marks the start of the relevant arm. It is important to take account of this because the knitting instructions for each hand refer to this start of round.

Knit in stocking stitch in rounds.

Lift the two sets of 5 stitches reserved for each arm from the stitch holders on to a set of needles.

Distribution of stitches: 3/2/3/2 [10 sts].

Rounds 1–4: Join into round and knit four rounds [10 sts]. These four rounds form the joint and should not be stuffed with wadding.

The yellow dot marks the starting point for the right arm.

The yellow dot marks the starting point for the left arm.

Round 5: K2, inc1, k6, inc1, k2 [12 sts].

Round 6 onwards: Knit in rounds until the desired length is reached. Pull the starting yarn slightly before finishing off, so that the stitches of the joining rows pull together a bit, making the stitches look nicer.

Arm chart

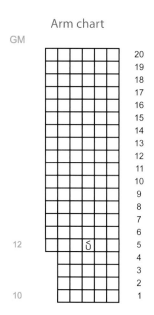

This chart shows half the stitches for the arm. Continue each round on the second pair of needles, working the chart in mirror image.

Knitting the Hands

There are four hand variations: hand without thumb, hand with thumb, four-fingered hand and hoofed hand. Any hand can be knitted on to any animal.

Hand without thumb

Round 1: * K1, inc1 *, repeat from * to * four more times, k1. Repeat once more from the beginning [22 sts].

Rounds 2–6: Knit.

Stuff the arm with wadding, avoiding stuffing in the area of the joint. Stuff the hand with wadding.

Round 7: K2tog, k7, k2tog twice, k7, k2tog [18 sts].

Round 8: K2tog, k5, k2tog twice, k5, k2tog [14 sts].

Round 9: K2tog, k3tog, k2tog twice, k3tog, k2tog [6 sts].

Before pulling together, stuff with some extra wadding, if necessary. Cut off the yarn, pull through the remaining stitches and finish off.

Chart for the hand without thumb

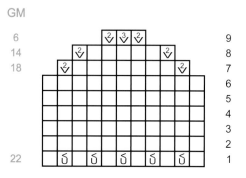

This chart shows half the stitches for the hand without a thumb. Repeat the stitches once each round.

Hand with thumb

Begin the hand as follows:

Round 1: * K1, inc1 *, repeat from * to * four more times, k1. Repeat once more from the beginning [22 sts].

Rounds 2–4: Knit.

Stuff the arm with wadding, avoiding stuffing in the area of the joint.

Thumb:

The first 3 and last 3 stitches of the round are knitted in rounds for the thumb. Leave the remaining stitches for now.

Rounds 1–2: Make into a round and knit [6 sts].

Round 3: K1, k2tog twice, k1 [4 sts].

Cut off the yarn and pull through the remaining 4 stitches. The thumb is complete.

For the **Hand**, continue knitting the remaining 16 stitches in rounds, starting with the stitches at the beginning of the first needle.

Rounds 5–7: Knit.

Stuff the hand with wadding.

Round 8: K2tog, k4, k2tog twice, k4, k2tog [12 sts].

Round 9: K2tog, k2, k2tog twice, k2, k2tog [8 sts].

Before pulling together, stuff with some extra wadding if necessary. Cut, leaving a long strand of yarn, and pull through the remaining stitches. Using the yarn, invisibly sew up the opening between the hand and thumb and finish off.

Chart for the hand with thumb

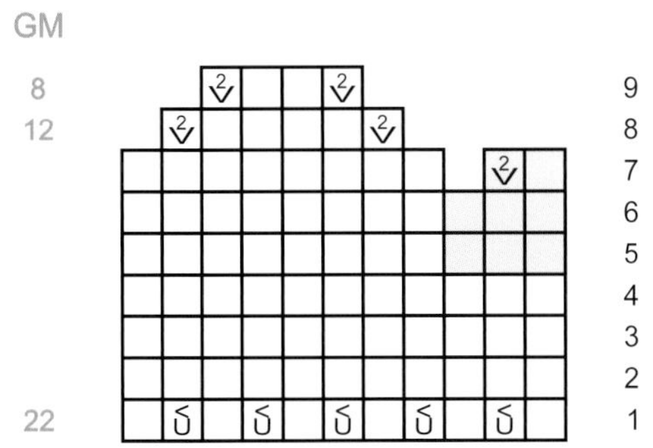

This chart shows half the stitches for the hand with a thumb. Continue each round on the second pair of needles, working the chart in mirror image.

Four-fingered hand

Work the hand as follows:

Round 1: * K1, inc1 *, repeat from * to * four more times, k1. Repeat once more from the beginning [22 sts].

Rounds 2–4: Knit.

Stuff the arm with wadding, avoiding stuffing the joint.

Thumb:

The first 3 and last 3 stitches of the round are knitted in rounds for the thumb. Leave the remaining stitches for now.

Rounds 1–2: Form into a round and knit [6 sts].

Round 3: K1, k2tog twice, k1 [4 sts].

Cut off the yarn and pull through the remaining 4 stitches. The thumb is complete. Stuff some wadding in the hand area and in the thumb.

Index finger:

The first 3 and last 3 stitches of the round are knitted in rounds as for the thumb. Leave the remaining stitches for now.

Rounds 1–3: Form into a round and knit [6 sts].

Round 4: K1, k2tog twice, k1 [4 sts].

Cut off the yarn and pull through the remaining 4 stitches. The index finger is complete.

Middle finger:

The first 3 and last 3 stitches of the round are knitted in rounds as for the thumb.

Rounds 1–3: Form into a round and knit [6 sts].

Round 4: K1, k2tog twice, k1 [4 sts].

Cut off the yarn and pull through the remaining 4 stitches. The middle finger is complete. Stuff some wadding in the finger and the hand area.

Little finger:

Work over the remaining 4 stitches in rounds.

Rounds 1–3: Form into a round and knit [4 sts].

Cut off the yarn and pull through all 4 stitches. The little finger is complete. Using the yarn, invisibly sew up the openings between the individual fingers and then finish off.

Hoofed Hand

Work as follows:

Round 1: * K1, inc1 *, repeat from * to * four more times, k1. Repeat once more from the beginning [22 sts].

Rounds 2–6: Knit.

Stuff the arm with wadding, avoiding the joint.

Stuff the hoof with wadding.

Round 7: Purl.

Round 8: K2tog five times, k2, k2tog five times [12 sts].

Round 9: Knit.

Round 10: K2tog to the end [6 sts].

Before pulling together, stuff with some extra wadding, if necessary. Cut off the yarn, pull through the remaining stitches and finish off.

Chart for the four-fingered hand

Chart for the hoofed hand

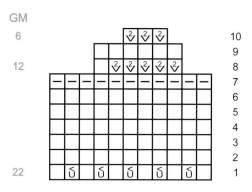

This chart shows half the stitches for the four-fingered hand. Continue each round on the second pair of needles, working the chart in mirror image.

This chart shows half the stitches for the hoofed hand. Continue each round on the second pair of needles, working the chart in mirror image.

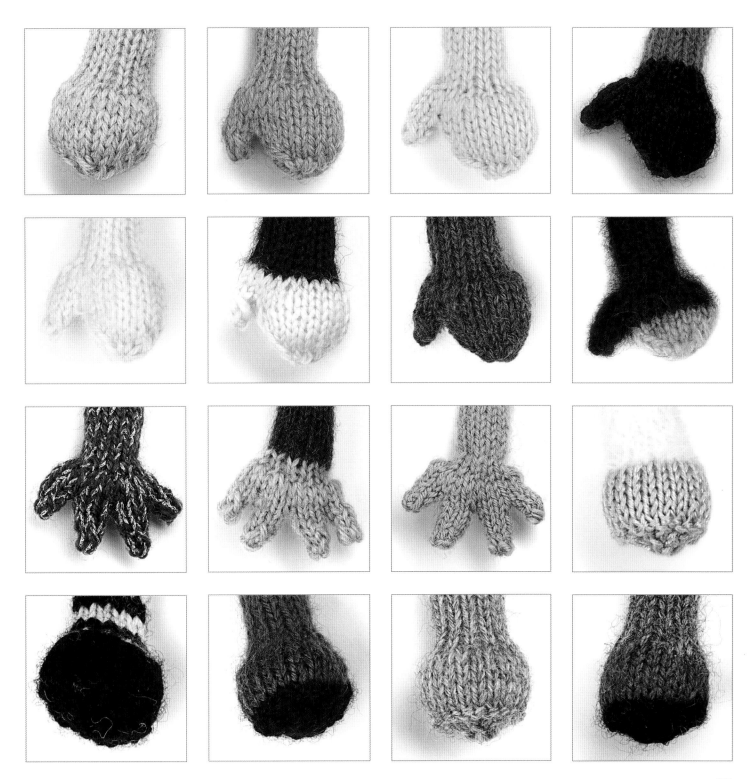

Knitting the Tail

Materials

- Yarn as listed for your chosen animal
- Set of 5 double-pointed knitting needles in the size specified in the pattern
- Wadding

Instructions for knitting each tail are provided in the individual project instructions but the following general information applies:

- The stitches for the relevant tail are created on the body pattern on rounds 15 and 18.
- The tail should be knitted before the body is stuffed.
- The two sets of 5 stitches left on the stitch holders for the tail should be transferred to a set of double-pointed needles. This is recommended, despite the small number of stitches involved.

- If the tail is stuffed with wadding, this is stated in the individual instructions.
- You can knit any tail on any of the animals. The mouse (page 30), for example, has been given the dog's tail.
- Four animals do not have tails, so no stitches are increased. This is specified in the individual instructions.

Knitting the Forehead

For some animals in this book, the forehead (which is combined with the sides of the face) is knitted first followed by the appropriate nose or snout. The forehead begins with two rounds and is then worked in short rows. The basic shape of the forehead is described here. For some animals there are variations.

Lift the stitches left on the stitch holders on to a set of needles – you have 9 stitches from the top back of the head plus the 17 stitches set aside in round 3 when you knitted the back of the head. These 17 stitches were originally arranged as 4/9/4. Arrange your stitches as 9/4/9/4 [26 sts].

Pick-up round: K9, pick up 8 stitches at the side, knit the remaining 17 stitches then pick up 8 stitches at the side. Redistribute the stitches as 9/12/9/12 [42 sts].

Round 1: Join into round and knit.

Round 2: Knit.

Round 3: Now knit in short rows, as follows, only working on the stitches of needles 1, 2 and 4. The stitches of needle 3 (under the chin) should be left on a stitch holder. Although you will be knitting several rows, for reference purposes we will call this round 3. This is the actual forehead.

Distribution of stitches:

12 (needle 2)/9 (needle 1)/12 (needle 4) [33 sts].

Start of row: 1st stitch of needle 1:

Row 1: K8, k2tog, turn work [11/9/12; 32 sts].

Row 2: P8, p2tog, turn work [11/9/11; 31 sts].

Row 3: K8, k2tog, turn work [10/9/11; 30 sts].

Row 4: P8, p2tog, turn work [10/9/10; 29 sts].

Forehead chart

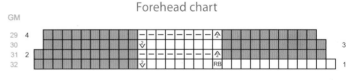

This chart shows the short-row shaping of the forehead. The stitches on the third needle (not included) are not used. The rounds begin at RB.

Round 4: Starting at the 1st stitch of needle 1, k8, k2tog, knit 9 + 9 + 9 stitches, knit together the last stitch on needle 4 with the 1st stitch on needle 1 for the 5th round [9/9/9/9; 36 sts].

Round 5: Knit.

Knitting a Big Nose

A large nose can be knitted on to any animal with a forehead, apart from the elephant. A dog could therefore have a large nose, rather than a standard nose. If he is given the dog's ears and tail, he will still be a dog.

Here are the instructions for the simplest form of the large nose. The other faces with large noses differ slightly.

Start knitting the large nose after completing the forehead, starting with the first stitch of the first needle.

Rounds 1–17: Knit [36 sts].

Stuff the body and the head with wadding.

Round 18: K1, k2tog, k3, k2tog, k1. Repeat on each needle [28 sts].

Round 19: Knit.

Round 20: K1, k2tog, k1, k2tog, k1. Repeat on each needle [20 sts].

Round 21: Knit.

Stuff the nose with wadding.

Round 22: K2tog, k1, k2tog. Repeat on each needle [12 sts].

Before pulling together, stuff with some extra wadding, if necessary.

Cut off the yarn, pull through the remaining stitches and finish off.

Big nose chart

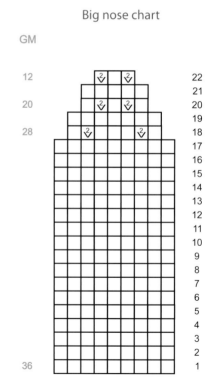

This chart shows the pattern for the stitches on one needle. Repeat on the other three needles.

Knitting a Mouse Face

This face is knitted directly after the back of the head – do not knit the forehead first. The modular approach means that any animal could be given this face. A dog could therefore have this face, rather than a dog's face. If he is given the dog's ears and tail, he will still be a dog.

Lift the stitches left on the stitch holders on to a set of needles – you have 9 stitches from the top back of the head plus 17 stitches set aside in round 3 when you knitted the back of the head. These 17 stitches were originally arranged as 4/9/4. Arrange your stitches as 9/4/9/4 [26 sts].

Pick-up round: K9, pick up 8 stitches at the side, knit the remaining 17 stitches, pick up 8 stitches at the side [9/12/9/12; 42 sts].

Start of round: 1st stitch of needle 1. In some rounds, this stitch is knitted together with the last stitch of needle 4 in the previous round.

Round 1: Join into a round and knit each stitch [42 sts].

Round 2: Knit to the last stitch (see round 3).

Round 3: Knit together the last stitch of needle 4 with the 1st stitch of needle 1, k7, k2tog, k9, k2tog, k9, k2tog, k9 [9/10/9/10; 38 sts].

Round 4: Knit.

Round 5: K19, k2tog, k5, k2tog, k10 [9/10/7/10; 36 sts].

Round 6: Knit to the last stitch (see round 7).

Round 7: Knit together the last stitch of needle 4 with the 1st stitch of needle 1, k7, k2tog, k7, k2tog, k7, k2tog, k7 [9/8/7/8; 32 sts].

Round 8: Knit to the last stitch (see round 9).

Round 9: Knit together the last stitch of needle 4 with the 1st stitch of needle 1, k7, k2tog, k8, k2tog, k1, k2tog, k8 [9/7/5/7; 28 sts].

Round 10: Knit.

Stuff the body and the head with wadding.

Round 11: K2tog, k5, k2tog, k5, k2tog, k5, k2tog, k5 [7/6/5/6; 24 sts].

Round 12: Knit.

Round 13: K2tog, k3, k2tog, k4, k2tog, k5, k2tog, k4 [5/5/5/5; 20 sts].

Rounds 14–16: Knit.

Round 17: K2tog, k1, k2tog twice, k11, k2tog [3/4/5/4; 16 sts].

Round 18: Knit.

Stuff the nose with wadding.

Round 19: K3, k2tog, k9, k2tog [3/3/5/3; 14 sts].

Round 20: Knit.

Before pulling together, stuff with some extra wadding, if necessary. Cut off the yarn and pull through the remaining stitches.

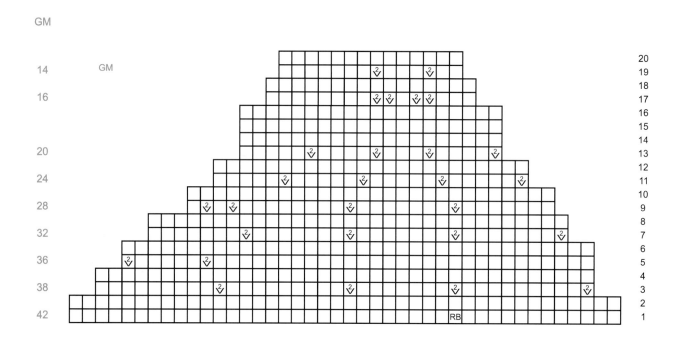

This chart for knitting the mouse face shows all the stitches in the sequence 4th, 1st, 2nd and 3rd needle, read from the right. Start knitting at the round beginning (RB).

26

Knitting the Ears

Materials

- Yarn as listed for your chosen animal
- Set of 5 double-pointed knitting needles in the size specified in the pattern
- Small crochet hook of the same size as the knitting needles

The ears are knitted individually for each animal. Some ears are knitted in rounds. Even if there are only a very few stitches, these ears are best knitted on a set of double-pointed needles. Other ears are knitted in rows. These are worked in two parts and then sewn or crocheted together.

The stitches are picked up at different places on the top or at the sides of the head, depending on which animal you are making. The exact positioning of the ears is described in the individual instructions for each animal, but this is only a guide. The ears can be positioned individually, if desired. Even the distance between the ears is an inexact science. For example, the large ears of the elephant could be knitted on to the mouse by increasing the number of stitches to be picked up.

In general, the following applies:

- The ears are never stuffed with wadding.
- Picking up stitches for the ears is different for each animal. The stitches are picked up in different places and at different angles depending on the animal being made.
- Generally you should pick up the stitches for the ears with the animal facing away from you.
- Start with the left ear.

Picking up stitches on the top and side of the head.

Knitting ears in the round:

1. Start where you want the top end of the left ear to be and then work outwards as explained here. With the back of the head towards you, use the crochet hook to reach through under a stitch in the stuffed head and pull through a loop of yarn. The first stitch created in this way should be pulled tight again in the same way. For the next stitch, pull a loop through under the next purl stitch in the knitting. Continue until you have picked up the desired number of stitches for half of the ear.
2. Distribute the stitches across two double-pointed knitting needles.
3. To pick up the second half of the stitches (front or inner ear), turn the animal round so it is facing you. Pick up the next stitches as close to the stitches for the outer ear as possible. Distribute these stitches over two knitting needles as before.

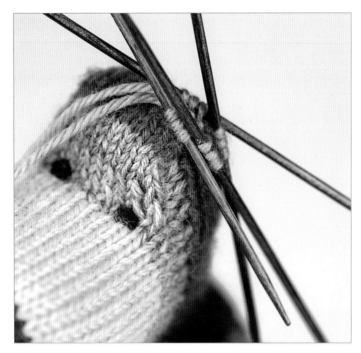

Picking up stitches for an ear that is knitted in rounds.

Picking up stitches at a right angle on the head.

4. Join the round and knit following the instructions for your chosen animal.
5. When picking up stitches for the right ear, start at the side of the head and continue upwards, then pick up the stitches on the head.
6. Pick up the second half of the stitches (front or inner ear), first at the top of the head, then downwards at the side of the head.

Knitting ears in rows

Pick up the stitches for the left ear as described in step 1 above. Knit the outer ear in stocking stitch as described in the instructions for your chosen animal. Pick up and knit the stitches for the inner ear right beside the outer ear. Pick up the stitches for the right ear following the instructions in step 5 above.

Picking up stitches on the head.

Embroidering Facial Details

The facial details, such as the eyes, nose and mouth, are embroidered on to the completed heads using embroidery cotton. For this, use two to four strands of embroidery cotton. Instructions for the cat's whiskers are given on page 86.

Embroidering the eyes

For most of the knitted animals, the eyes are about 4–5mm (a scant ¼in) wide and 3–5mm (⅛–¼in) high. The width of the eyes corresponds roughly to the width of 1.5–2 knitting stitches, but you can, of course, make the eyes whatever size you like. Usually the eyes are embroidered with black or brown embroidery thread although the cat, for example (page 84), has green eyes. Work the eyes as follows:

1. Knot the embroidery thread and insert the needle from the back of the head through to the desired position on the face at the bottom edge of one eye. Make a horizontal stitch the desired width of the eye and bring the needle out just above the start of the first stitch.

2. Work in satin stitch. Make two or three more stitches, working upwards. Now shape the eye by working a narrower stitch and then an even narrower one, so that the eye tapers upwards. The eye can also be made using four or five stitches of the same width. When you are finished, knot off the thread and pass the needle through to the back where the thread end can be cut off.

Embroidering the nose

Embroider the nose with satin stitch as you did for the eyes. Start at the widest point of the nose and work two stitches. Work a pair of narrower stitches, and then work another pair of even narrower stitches until the nose is the desired depth. As with the eyes, you can change the length and number of stitches to suit the animal and your personal preference.

Embroidering the mouth

For the mouth simply work a few long straight stitches using two strands of thread. Refer to the photographs of your chosen animal as your guide.

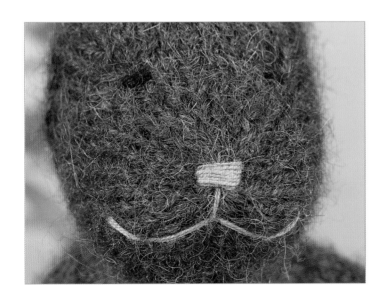

PAULIE PUPPY & MAXINE MOUSE

PAULIE & MAXINE

Materials

- A total of about 25g (1oz) sock yarn (80% super merino, 20% nylon) in assorted colours
- Black embroidery cotton
- About 10g (½oz) wadding
- Set of 2.5mm (UK 12/US 2) double-pointed knitting needles

Knitting these two characters will help you learn how the animals are put together. The happy pair is knitted in assorted colours to highlight the different stages of assembly but you can choose your own colour(s) as desired.

Method

The torso and back of the head:

For a multi-coloured animal, work in your main colour. Knit the torso following the instructions on pages 10–12 and then knit the back of the head following the instructions on page 13.

The lower limbs:

Knit each leg for 20 rounds following the instructions on page 14. The first four rounds can be knitted in a separate colour to highlight the joint. Finish with the standard foot (see pages 14–16).

The upper limbs:

Knit each arm for 20 rounds following the instructions on pages 17–18. As with the legs, you can knit the first four rounds in a separate colour. On Maxine Mouse, finish with the hands with thumbs (pages 18–19) and for Paulie Puppy, finish with the hands without thumbs (page 18).

The tail:

Both animals have the dog's tail (see the photo on page 9). Follow the instructions for making this tail on pages 88–89.

The face:

Maxine Mouse has a traditional mouse face. Knit this following the instructions on pages 25–26.
Paulie Puppy has a forehead and big nose. Knit these following the instructions on pages 23 and 24. Change colour for each section, if desired.
Embroider the small eyes and the tip of Maxine Mouse's nose using black embroidery cotton (see page 29).

The ears:

Maxine Mouse has two-piece mouse ears. Follow the instructions on page 42 to make these.
Paulie Puppy has dog's ears. You'll find instructions for these on page 90.

ROSIE PIG & MICKEY MONKEY

Pig • About 15cm (6in) high | Monkey • About 19cm (7½in) high

ROSIE PIG

Materials

- About 25g (1oz) pink sock yarn (80% super merino, 20% nylon)
- Dark-brown embroidery cotton for the eyes
- About 10g (½oz) wadding
- Set of 2.25mm (UK 13/US 1) double-pointed knitting needles

Method

The torso:

Knit the torso following the instructions on pages 10–11 up to the end of round 42 [28 sts] then continue as follows:

Round 43: K7, k2tog, k3, k2tog, k7, k2tog, k3, k2tog [7/5/7/5; 24 sts]. The body ends here – Rosie does not have a neck.

The back of the head:

Leave the 7 stitches on needle 3 aside for the face. Knit the stitches on needles 1, 2 and 4 as follows:

Start of row: 1st stitch of needle 1.

Row 1: K1, inc1, k5, inc1, k1, k5. (This takes you up to the end of needle 2.) Turn work [5/9/5; 19 sts].

Row 2: Purl all stitches (including the stitches on needle 4). Turn work.

Row 3 onwards: Continue as instructed for the back of the head (page 13) from row 6 onwards.

Lower limbs:

Knit the legs for 15 rounds each and follow with the standard foot (see pages 14–16).

Upper limbs:

Knit the arms for 18 rounds each and follow with the hand with thumb (see pages 17–19).

The curly tail:

Knit the tail in rounds and then short rows as instructed here:

Round 1: Join the two sets of 5 stitches set aside for the tail into a round and knit.

Rounds 2–5: Knit.

Round 6: K2tog, k3, k2tog, k3 [8 sts].

Now there is some short-row shaping:

Row 7: K7, turn work.

Row 8: P6, turn work.

Row 9: K5, turn work.

Row 10: P4, turn work.

Row 11: K4, k2tog [7 sts].

Row 12: K2tog, k3, turn work [6 sts].

Row 13: P3, turn work.

Row 14: K2, k2tog, turn work [5 sts].

Row 15: P3, turn work.

Row 16: K2, k2tog [4 sts].

Row 17: K2tog, k2 [3 sts].

Row 18: P1, turn work.

Row 19: K2tog [2 sts].

Cut off the yarn and pull through the remaining stitches. Pull the yarn through at the side of the little tail and use mattress stitch, pulled tightly, to make the tail curl a little more. Do not stuff the tail with wadding.

The face:

Take the 9 stitches left at the top of the back of the head and put them on needle 1. Lift the 7 stitches left on a stitch holder when you began the back of the head (see above) and put them on needle 3.

Pick-up round:

Needle 1: K9.

Needle 2: Pick up and knit 12 stitches at the side.

Needle 3: K1, pick up 1 stitch, k5, pick up 1 stitch, k1.

Needle 4: Pick up and knit 12 stitches at the side. Close into a round [9/12/9/12; 42 sts].

Rounds 1–5: Work the forehead (see page 23) [9/9/9/9; 36 sts].

Round 6: K1, k2tog, k3, k2tog, k11, k2tog, k3, k2tog, k10 [7/9/7/9; 32 sts].

Rounds 7–9: Knit.

Round 10: K8, k2tog, k3, k2tog, k9, k2tog, k3, k2tog, k1 [7/7/7/7; 28 sts].

Rounds 11–13: Knit.

Stuff the body, head and nose with wadding.

Round 14: * K1, k2tog, k1, k2tog, k1 *, repeat from * to * three more times [5/5/5/5; 20 sts].

Rounds 15–18: Knit.

Round 19: Purl (nose 'rim').

Round 20: * K1, k2tog, k2 *, repeat from * to * three more times [4/4/4/4; 16 sts].

Rounds 21–22: Knit.

Round 23: * K1, k2tog, k1 *, repeat from * to * three more times [3/3/3/3; 12 sts].

Before pulling together, stuff with some extra wadding, if necessary. Cut off the yarn and pull through the remaining stitches. Use the yarn to shape the circle of the nose 'rim' worked in round 19, ensuring that it does not bulge out.

You can now embroider Rosie's small eyes using dark-brown embroidery cotton (see page 29).

This chart shows the stitches for Rosie's face from round 6. The chart for the previous rounds (the forehead) is on page 23.

Face chart

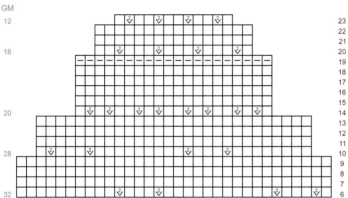

Left ear:

Pick-up round: Referring to the instructions on pages 27–28, pick up 3 stitches on the top of the head, 5 stitches at the side, then 5 stitches back up the side and 3 stitches on the top of the head. Refer to the photographs opposite to help you see where to pick up the stitches.

Round 1: Join the stitches into a round and knit [16 sts].
Rounds 2–7: Knit.
Round 8: K6, k2tog twice, k6 [14 sts].
Round 9: Knit.

Round 10: K2tog, k10, k2tog [12 sts].
Round 11: Knit.
Round 12: K2tog, k8, k2tog [10 sts].
Round 13: Knit.
Round 14: K2tog, k1, k2tog twice, k1, k2tog [6 sts].
Round 15: Knit.
Round 16: K3tog twice.

Cut off the yarn and pull through the remaining stitches. Bend the ear over roughly at a 90° angle and invisibly sew the top part down.

Right ear:

Pick-up round: Pick up 5 stitches at the side of the head, level with the first ear, and 3 stitches on the top of the head, then turn and pick up 3 stitches on the top of the head and 5 stitches at the side. Knit the right ear in the same way as the left one, remembering that the ears should be symmetrical.

This chart shows the stitches for half of Rosie's ear. Continue each round on the second pair of needles, working the chart in mirror image.

Ear chart

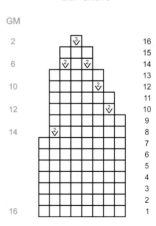

MICKEY MONKEY

Materials

- About 25g (1oz) dark-brown sock yarn (80% super merino, 20% nylon)
- About 10g (½oz) beige sock yarn (80% super merino, 20% nylon)
- Dark-brown embroidery cotton for the eyes
- About 10g (½oz) wadding
- Set of 2.5mm (UK 12/US 2) double-pointed knitting needles

Method

The torso and back of the head:

Using dark-brown sock yarn, work following the instructions for the torso, rounds 1–42 on pages 10–12 but do not create any stitches in round 15 or 18 for a tail. Mickey has a short neck and no tail.
Knit the back of the head directly after the body (see page 13).

The lower limbs:

Mickey has longer than average arms and legs. Make each leg 6cm (2½in) long, knitting 28 rounds following the instructions on page 14 and using dark-brown yarn [16 sts]. You can, of course, make longer or shorter legs if preferred.
Finish with the standard foot using beige yarn (see pages 15–16).

The upper limbs:

Mickey's arms with hands are 7.5cm (3in) long. Work each one as follows:
Rounds 1–26: Using dark-brown yarn, knit 26 rounds for the arms following the instructions on pages 17–18 [10 sts].
Rounds 27–30: Change to beige yarn and knit four more rounds. Finish with the four-fingered hand using beige yarn (see pages 19–20).

The forehead and face:

Lift the stitches left on the stitch holders on to a set of needles.
Rounds 1–2: Using dark-brown yarn, knit the first two rounds of the forehead (page 23) [9/12/9/12; 42 sts].
Round 3 (short-row shaping): Change to the beige yarn. Knit the short rows of the forehead (round 3) and continue in the same way until the distribution of stitches is 8/9/8 [25 sts] (plus 9 left on the stitch holder).

This chart shows the short-row shaping of Mickey's forehead. The stitches on the third needle (not included) are placed on a stitch holder. RB marks the beginning.

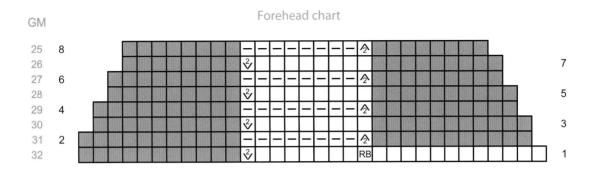

Forehead chart

Start of round: 1st stitch of needle 1. Continue on from the forehead.

Round 4: K8, k2tog, knit to the last stitch then knit this together with the 1st stitch of needle 1 [9/7/9/7; 32 sts].

Round 5: Knit.

The stitches must now be redistributed so you can work the mouth. Do this as you knit.

Round 6:

Needle 1: Knit the last 3 stitches of needle 4, the 9 stitches of needle 1 plus the first 3 stitches of needle 2 [15 sts].

Needle 2: Inc1, k1, inc1 [3 sts].

Needle 3: Knit the 3 remaining stitches from needle 2, the 9 stitches of needle 3 and then the first 3 stitches of needle 4 [15 sts].

Needle 4: Inc1, k1, inc1 [3 sts].

Distribution of stitches: 15/3/15/3 [36 sts].

Round 7: * K1, inc1, k6, inc1, k1, inc1, k6, inc1, k4 *, repeat from * to * once more [19/3/19/3; 44 sts].

Rounds 8–9: Knit.

Round 10: * K1, k2tog, k13, k2tog, k4 *, repeat from * to * once more [17/3/17/3; 40 sts].

Round 11: Knit.

Round 12: * K1, k2tog, k11, k2tog, k4 *, repeat from * to * once more [15/3/15/3; 36 sts].

Round 13: Knit.

Round 14: * K1, k2tog, k9, k2tog, k1, k3tog *, repeat from * to * once more [13/1/13/1; 28 sts].

Round 15: Knit.

Stuff the body and head with wadding.

Round 16: * K2tog, k2, k2tog, k1, k2tog, k2, k2tog, k1 *, repeat from * to * once more [9/1/9/1; 20 sts].

Redistribute the 20 stitches over two needles by adding the single stitch on needle 2 to the end of needle 1 and the single stitch on needle 4 to the end of needle 3. We will now call the needles with stitches needle 1 and needle 2. Add further stuffing as needed before casting off completely.

Cast off: Lift the last stitch of needle 2 over the 1st stitch of needle 1, slip. Lift what is now the 1st stitch of needle 1 on to needle 2, knit this stitch together with the following stitch on needle 2, then lift the 1st stitch of the right (working) needle over, lift this on to the right needle. Keep working in this way until all the stitches have been cast off.

Embroider the eyes using dark-brown embroidery cotton (see page 29).

The left outer ear:

The ears are worked in stocking stitch in two parts and then invisibly sewn together.

Pick-up round: With the back of the head facing you, pick up and knit 8 stitches in dark brown on the third row of stitches at the side of the head (or wherever you think looks right).

Row 1: Purl [8 sts].

Row 2: K1, inc1, k6, inc1, knit 1 [10 sts].

Row 3: Purl.

Row 4: K1, k2tog, k4, k2tog, knit 1 [8 sts].

Row 5: P1, p2tog, p2, p2tog, p1 [6 sts].

Row 6: K2tog, k2, k2tog [4 sts].

Cast off the stitches purlwise.

Sew the inner ear invisibly to the outer ear with beige yarn.

This chart shows all the stitches for Mickey's outer ear.

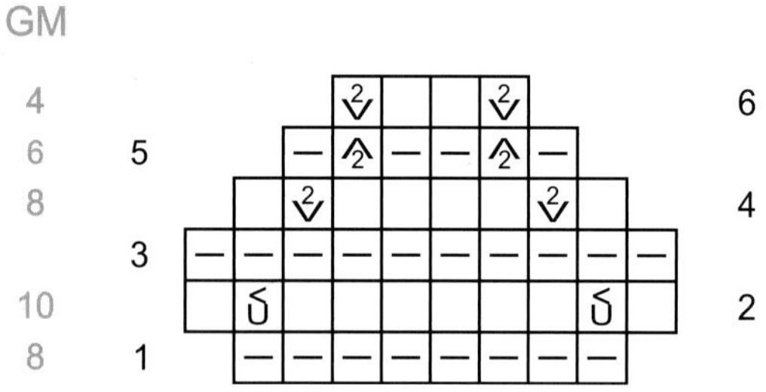

The left inner ear:

Turn the monkey so he is facing you.

Pick-up round: Pick up and knit 7 stitches in beige directly next to the front edge of the outer ear.

Row 1: Purl (wrong-side row) [7 sts].

Row 2: Knit.

Row 3: Purl.

Row 4: K2tog, k3, k2tog [5 sts].

Cast off the stitches purlwise.

The right ear:

Pick up and knit the stitches for the right ear in the same way.

This chart shows all the stitches for Mickey's inner ear.

Outer ear chart

GM

Inner ear chart

GM

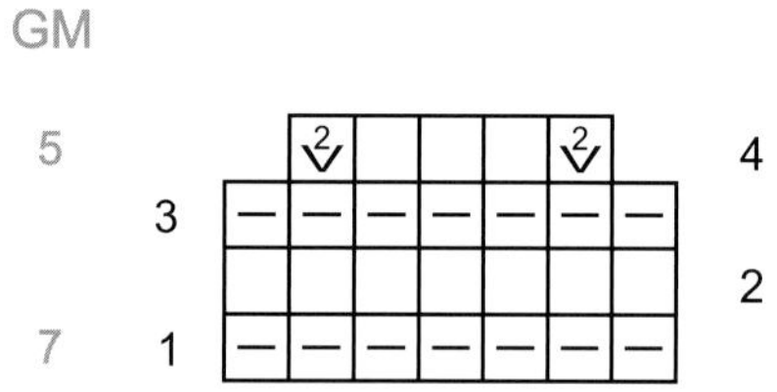

MEL MOUSE & EDWARD ELEPHANT

MEL MOUSE

Materials

- About 25g (1oz) brown sock yarn (80% super merino, 20% nylon)
- Embroidery cotton in black and light pink for the eyes and nose
- About 10g (½oz) wadding
- Set of 2.25mm (UK 13/US 1) double-pointed knitting needles

Method

The torso and back of the head:

Knit the 47 rounds of the torso following the instructions on pages 10–12 then knit the back of the head (see page 13).

The lower limbs:

Knit each leg for 15 rounds following the instructions on page 14 and finish with the standard foot (pages 15–16).

The upper limbs:

Knit each arm for 15 rounds following the instructions on pages 17–18 and finish with the hand with thumb (pages 18–19).

The tail:

The tail is not stuffed with wadding.

Transfer the two sets of 5 stitches left on stitch holders on to a set of needles.

Knit in rounds for about 6cm (2½in) [10 sts].

Next round: K2tog, k8 [9 sts].

Knit for 2cm (¾in).

Next round: K2tog, k7 [8 sts].

Knit for 2cm (¾in).

Next round: K2tog twice, k4 [6 sts].

Next round: Knit.

Cut off the yarn, pull through the remaining stitches and finish off.

The face:

Knit the mouse face following the instructions on pages 25–26. Embroider the eyes in black and the nose in pink (see page 29).

The left ear:

Refer to the instructions on pages 27–28.

Pick-up round: With the mouse facing you, pick up 4 stitches on the top of the head and then 7 stitches at the side. Turn the mouse around and work your way back on the other side, picking up 7 stitches at the side and 4 stitches on the top of the head [22 sts].

Round 1: Join into a round and knit.

Round 2: K1, inc1, k20, inc1, k1 [24 sts].

Round 3: * K1, inc1, k10, inc1, k1 *, repeat from * to * once more [28 sts].

Round 4: Knit.

Round 5: * K1, inc1, k12, inc1, k1 *, repeat from * to * once more [32 sts].

Rounds 6–9: Knit.

Round 10: * K2tog, k12, k2tog *, repeat from * to * once more [28 sts].

Round 11: * K2tog, k10, k2tog *, repeat from * to * once more [24 sts].

Round 12: * K2tog, k8, k2tog *, repeat from * to * once more [20 sts].

Round 13: * K2tog, k6, k2tog *, repeat from * to * once more [16 sts].

Round 14: * K2tog, k4, k2tog *, repeat from * to * once more [12 sts].

Then cast off the remaining stitches together.

The right ear:

Pick-up round: With the mouse facing you, pick up 7 stitches at the side of the head and 4 stitches on the top. Turn the mouse around and work your way back on the other side, picking up 4 stitches on the top of the head and 7 stitches at the side. Knit the right ear in the same way as the left one.

This chart shows half the stitches for Mel's ear. Continue each round on the second pair of needles, working the chart in mirror image.

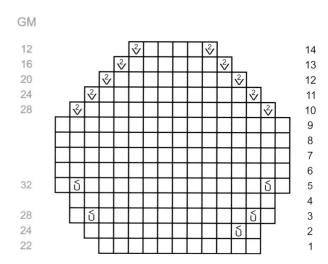

Ear chart

EDWARD ELEPHANT

Materials

- About 30g (1oz) light-grey sock yarn (80% super merino, 20% nylon)
- About 50cm (20in) dark-grey or black sock yarn for the tassel at the end of the tail (80% super merino, 20% nylon) or you can use the light grey sock yarn
- Black embroidery cotton
- About 10g (½oz) wadding
- Set of 2.25mm (UK 13/US 1) double-pointed knitting needles

Method

The torso:

The elephant has a fat tummy so the torso needs adjustment as follows:

Rounds 1–20: Work following the torso pattern, rounds 1–20 on pages 10–11.

Distribution of stitches: 13/12/13/12 [50 sts].

Round 21: K27, inc1, k2, inc1, k2, inc1, k1, inc1, k2, inc1, k2, inc1, k2, k12 [13/12/19/12; 56 sts].

Rounds 22–30: Knit.

Round 31: K25, * k1, k2tog *, repeat from * to * five more times, k1, k12 [13/12/13/12; 50 sts].

Rounds 32–47: Continue as for the torso pattern (rounds 32–47) on pages 11–12.

The back of the head:

Work the back of the head directly on to the torso following the instructions on page 13.

The legs:

The elephant has chunky legs.

Rounds 1–4: Knit the first four rounds for the leg pattern on page 14 [12 sts].

Round 5: * K1, inc1, k2, inc1, k2, inc1, k1 *, repeat from * to * once more [18 sts].

Rounds 6–18: Knit.

The feet:

Round 1: * K1, inc1 *, repeat from * to * six more times, k2. Repeat from the beginning once more [32 sts].

Rounds 2–15: Work as for the hooves (page 16), but without increasing in round 4.

The upper limbs:

Knit each arm for 20 rounds following the instructions on pages 17–18 and then finish with the hoofed hand (page 20).

The tail:

Transfer the two sets of 5 stitches on the stitch holders to a set of needles.

Round 1: Join into a round and knit [10 sts].

Rounds 2–3: Knit.

Round 4: K1, k2tog, k4, k2tog, k1 [8 sts].

Rounds 5–6: Knit.

Round 7: K1, k2tog, k2, k2tog, k1 [6 sts].

Rounds 8–10: Knit.

Cut off the yarn and pull through the remaining stitches; do not pull tight. Wind some dark-grey or black sock yarn a few times around two fingers. Wind the yarn around the loops at one side, pull the yarn tight and place in the end of the little tail. Pull the stitches tight and fasten off the yarn.

This chart shows half the stitches for Edward's tail. Continue each round on the second pair of needles, working the chart in mirror image.

Tail chart

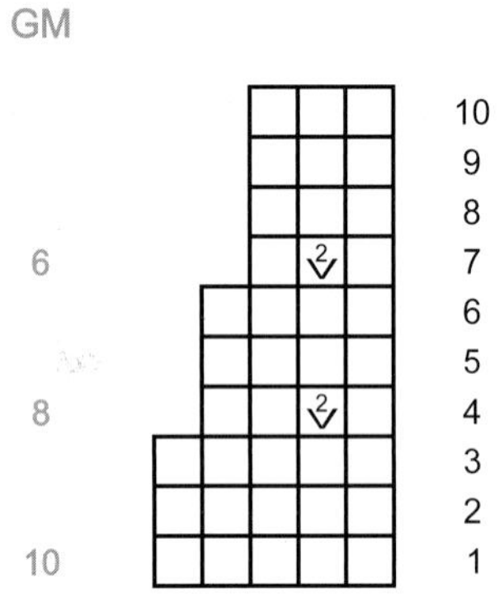

GM

The face:

Rounds 1–5: Knit the forehead following the instructions on page 23 [9/9/9/9; 36 sts].

Stuff the body and head with wadding.

Now knit the trunk as explained here, starting with short-row shaping.

Start point: 1st stitch of needle 1.

Round 1: K4, kfb, inc1, k4, turn work [11/9/9/9; 38 sts].

Round 2: P11, turn work.

Round 3: K5, inc2, k4, k3tog, turn work [13/7/9/9; 38 sts].

Round 4: P12, p3tog, turn work [13/7/9/7; 36 sts].

Round 5: K13, turn work.

Round 6: P13, turn work.

Round 7: K21, k2tog, k3, k2tog, k8 [13/7/7/7; 34 sts].

Round 8: K5, p1, k1, p1, k5, turn work.

Round 9: P13, turn work.

Round 10: K12, k2tog, k2tog, turn work [12/6/7/7; 32 sts].

Stuff wadding into the trunk knitted so far. Add further stuffing at intervals as you go along.

Round 11: P12, p2tog, turn work [12/6/7/6; 31 sts].

Round 12: Knit all stitches.

Round 13: K1, k2tog, k5, k2tog, k1, k2tog, k3, k2tog, k2, k2tog, k2, k2tog, k3, k2tog [9/5/5/5; 24 sts].

Round 14 incorporates more short-row shaping.

Round 14: k4, p1 k1, turn work. K4, turn work. P5, turn work. K6, turn work. P7, turn work. K8, k2tog (needle 2), k3, turn work. P13, p2tog (needle 4), turn work.

Round 15: Knit all stitches [9/4/5/4; 22 sts].

Round 16: Knit all stitches.

Round 17: K13, turn work.

Round 18: P17, turn work.

Round 19: K17, k2tog, turn work [9/4/4/4; 21 sts].

Round 20: P18, p2tog (needle 3), turn work [9/4/3/4; 20 sts].

Rounds 21–30: Knit all stitches.

Round 31: K2tog, k5, k2tog, k11 [7/4/3/4; 18 sts].

Rounds 32–36: Knit all stitches.

Round 37: K2tog, k3, k2tog, k11 [5/4/3/4; 16 sts].

Rounds 38–42: Knit all stitches.

Round 43: K2tog, k1, k2tog, k11 [3/4/3/4; 14 sts].

Rounds 44–48: Knit all stitches.

Round 49: Purl all stitches.

Round 50: K3tog, k2tog twice, k3tog, k2tog twice [1/2/1/2; 6 sts].

Cut off the yarn, pull through the remaining stitches and fasten off.

Embroider the eyes using black embroidery cotton (see page 29).

The left ear:

Pick-up round: With the elephant facing you, and referring to the instructions on pages 27–28, pick up 4 stitches on the top of the head and 12 stitches at the side. Turn the elephant away from you and work your way back on the other side, picking up 12 stitches at the side of the head and 4 stitches on the top [32 sts].

Round 1: Join into a round and knit [32 sts].

Round 2: Knit.

Round 3: * K1, inc1, k14, inc1, k1 *, repeat from * to * once more [36 sts].

Round 4: Knit.

Round 5: * K1, inc1, k16, inc1, k1 *, repeat from * to * once more [40 sts].

Round 6: Knit.

Round 7: * K1, inc1, k18, inc1, k1 *, repeat from * to * once more [44 sts].

Rounds 8–12: Knit.

Round 13: * k2tog, k18, k2tog *, repeat from * to * once more [40 sts].

Round 14: Knit.

Round 15: * K2tog, k16, k2tog *, repeat from * to * once more [36 sts].

Round 16: Knit.

Round 17: * K2tog, k14, k2tog *, repeat from * to * once more [32 sts].

Round 18: Knit.

Round 19: * K2tog, k1, k2tog, k1, k2tog *, repeat from * to * three more times [20 sts].

Round 20: Knit.

Round 21: K2tog 10 times [10 sts].

Cast off the remaining stitches together.

The right ear:

Pick-up round: With the elephant facing you, pick up 12 stitches at the side of the head and 4 stitches on the top. Turn the elephant away from you and then work your way back on the other side, picking up 4 stitches on the top of the head and 12 stitches at the side.

Knit the right ear in the same way as the left ear.

This chart shows half the stitches for Edward's ear. Repeat the stitches once on each round.

Ear chart

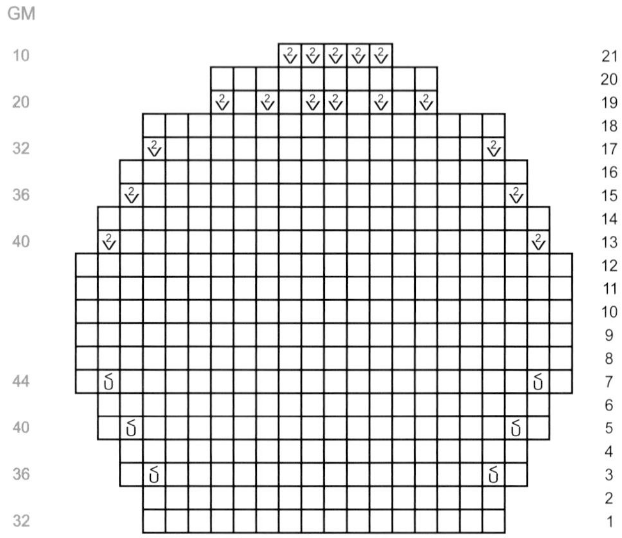

FREDDIE FROG & MATTY MOLE

FREDDIE FROG

Materials

- About 25g (1oz) light-green sock yarn (75% super merino, 25% polyamide)
- Black embroidery cotton
- About 10g (½oz) wadding
- Set of 2.25mm (UK 13/US 1) double-pointed knitting needles

Method

The torso and back of the head:

Knit rounds 1–45 for the torso following the instructions on pages 10–12 but do not create any stitches for a tail in round 15 or 18 – Freddie has a short neck and no tail.

Now knit the back of the head following the instructions on page 13.

The lower limbs:

The legs should be extra long and thin.

Knit each leg following the instructions on page 14 without increasing stitches in round 5 [12 sts] and working a total of 30 rounds.

Work the feet as follows:

Round 1: * K1, inc1, k2, inc1, k2, inc1, k1 *, repeat from * to * once more [18 sts].

Rounds 2–18: Follow the instructions for the standard foot on pages 15–16.

The upper limbs:

Knit each arm as instructed on pages 17–18, but finishing after 15 rounds. Then work the four-fingered hand (see pages 19–20).

The face:

Start of round: 1st stitch of the 4 stitches left on the stitch holder/4th needle.

The face is knitted in stocking stitch.

Pick-up round: K4 from the stitch holder, pick up 8 stitches at the side, k9, pick up 8 stitches at the side, k4 from stitch holder, k9 [12/9/12/9; 42 sts].

Round 2: K2tog, k29, k2tog. Leave the remaining 9 stitches on the needle [11/9/11; 31 sts]. Turn work.

Round 3: P2tog, p27, p2tog, turn work [10/9/10; 29 sts].

Round 4: K2tog, k25, k2tog, k9 [9/9/9; 36 sts].

Knit 5 stitches on needle 1 then redistribute the stitches as follows:

Needle 1: Knit the remaining 4 stitches on needle 1, the 9 stitches of needle 2 and the first 5 stitches of needle 3 [18 sts].

Needle 2: Knit the remaining 4 stitches of needle 3, the 9 stitches of needle 4 and the first 5 stitches of needle 1 [18 sts].

Round 5: Knit all stitches.

Stuff the body and the head with wadding.

In rounds 6–10, the stitches of needle 1 are always knitted three times in each round: knit the stitches, turn work, purl the stitches, turn work, knit the stitches, decreasing in the first knitted right-side row. (This makes the top of the face longer than the bottom to give it the characteristic froggy look.) Next, the stitches of needle 2 are knitted. The stitches of needle 2 are knitted just once in each round in the usual way; the same decreasing applies.

Round 6:

Needle 1: K1, k2tog, k12, k2tog, k1, turn work, p16, turn work, k16.

Needle 2: K1, k2tog, k12, k2tog, k1 [32 sts].

Round 7:

Needle 1: K1, k2tog, k10, k2tog, k1, turn work, p14, turn work, k14.

Needle 2: K1, k2tog, k10, k2tog, k1 [28 sts].

Round 8:

Needle 1: K1, k2tog, k8, k2tog, k1, turn work, p12, turn work, k12.

Needle 2: K1, k2tog, k8, k2tog, k1 [24 sts].

Round 9:

Needle 1: K1, k2tog, k6, k2tog, k1, turn work, p10, turn work, k10.

Needle 2: K1, k2tog, k6, k2tog, k1 [20 sts].

Stuff with wadding.

Round 10:

Needle 1: K1, k2tog, k4, k2tog, k1, turn work, p8, turn work, k8.

Needle 2: K1, k2tog, k6, k2tog, k1 [16 sts].

Round 11:

Needle 1: K1, k2tog, k2, k2tog, k1.

Needle 2: K1, k2tog, k2, k2tog, k1 [12 sts].

Before pulling together, stuff with some extra wadding, if necessary.

Break off the yarn, pull through the remaining stitches and finish off.

The left eye bulge:

The stitches for the eye bulges are picked up in a 'soft triangle' so that they can be stuffed with wadding. Pick up a total of 20 stitches as shown in the diagram. To do this, start with the frog facing you and begin by picking up the 8 stitches directly at the edge of the heel turn from bottom to top, then pick up 4 stitches slightly staggered, then 4 stitches parallel to the first stitches, then 4 stitches slightly staggered, so that you are back at the 1st stitch.

Round 1: Join into a round and knit [20 sts].

Rounds 2–3: Knit.

Round 4: K2tog, k4, k2tog twice, k8, k2tog [16 sts].

This chart shows the pattern for Freddie's face, starting at round 5.

Round 5: K2tog, k2, k2tog twice, k2, k2tog, k2, k2tog [11 sts].
Stuff the eye bulge with wadding.

Round 6: K2tog three times, k3tog, k2tog [5 sts].
Cut off the yarn, pull through the remaining stitches and finish off.

Chart for picking up the eye stitches

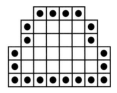

The right eye bulge:

Work as for the left eye bulge.

The pupils:

Embroider the pupil in black directly in the centre of each eye bulge at the edge leading to the mouth.

This chart shows all the stitches for each of Freddie's eye bulges.

Face chart

Needle 1

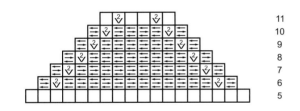

Needle 2

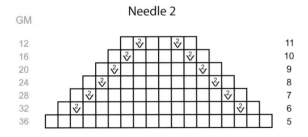

Eye bulge chart

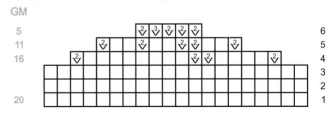

MATTY MOLE

Materials

- About 35g (1¼oz) black sock yarn (75% pure new wool, 25% polyamide)
- About 5g (less than ¼oz) pink sock yarn (75% pure new wool, 25% polyamide)
- About 10g (½oz) fine black mohair yarn (65% super kid mohair, 30% polyamide, 5% pure new wool)
- Embroidery thread in black and light pink
- About 10g (½oz) wadding
- Set of 2.5mm (UK 12/US 2) double-pointed knitting needles

Method

The mole is knitted with one strand of black sock yarn and one strand of fine mohair yarn in black.

The torso and back of the head:

Rounds 1–32: Work following the instructions for the torso, rounds 1–32 on pages 10–11 but do not create the extra stitches in round 15 or 18 for the tail.

Rounds 33–35: Knit (these rounds extend the body slightly).

Rounds 36–47: Now return to the instructions on pages 11–12 and finish the torso starting back at round 33 and working to round 44 – the mole has a short neck.

Directly afterwards, knit the back of the head (page 13).

The lower limbs:

The mole has very short legs. Work as follows for each leg:

Round 1: Join into a round and knit [12 sts].

Rounds 2–3: Knit.

Round 4: * K1, inc1, k4, inc1, k1*, repeat from * to * once more [16 sts].

Rounds 5–6: Knit.

Round 7: K4, inc1, k8, inc1, k4 [18 sts].

Round 8: Knit.

Knit a standard foot directly on to the bottom of each leg, starting at round 2 (see pages 15–16).

This chart shows half the stitches for each of Matty's legs. Continue each round on the second pair of needles, working the chart in mirror image.

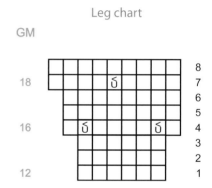

Leg chart

The upper limbs:

Knit each arm for 15 rounds following the instructions on pages 17–18. Finish with the hand with thumb (pages 18–19), working rounds 1–4 and the stitches for the thumb in black; knit the rest of the hand in pink. Either lightly stuff the arm with wadding or do not stuff it at all, but do stuff the hand.

The face:

Knit the mouse face following the instructions on pages 25–26. Embroider the eyes (see page 29), using black embroidery cotton and pulling the stitches firmly into the head to make little hollows. Embroider the nose in light pink embroidery cotton (see page 29).

ZOE ZEBRA & LARRY LION

ZOE ZEBRA

Materials

- About 15g (½oz) each of sock yarn in black and white (80% super merino, 20% nylon)
- Black embroidery cotton
- About 10g (½oz) wadding
- Set of 2.25mm (UK 13/US 1) double-pointed knitting needles

Method

Create the striped torso of the zebra by alternating three rounds in black with three rounds in white. For the back of the head, arms, legs, tail and face, alternate two rounds in black with two rounds in white. The hooves, the ears and end of the nose should be knitted in black.

The torso and back of the head:
Knit the torso following the instructions on pages 10–12, beginning with white and changing colour after every three rounds. Stop at the end of round 45, also in white.
Now knit the back of the head, referring to the instructions below and on page 13.
Round 1: Knit in black.
Round 2: Skip this round.

Round 3: Knit in black and divide up the stitches.
Row 4: Knit in black.
Rows 5–6: Knit in white.
Rows 7–28: Knit following the instructions on page 13, alternating the colours after every two rows.

The lower limbs:
Knit each leg following the instructions on page 14 and using the colours given below:
Round 1: Black.
Rounds 2–3: White.
Rounds 4–27: Continue to knit two rounds with each colour. Remember to increase in the fifth round [6 sts].
Knit the hoof in black straight on to each leg (see page 16).

The upper limbs:
Knit each arm following the instructions on pages 17–18 and using the colours given below:
Round 1: Black.
Rounds 2–3: White.
Rounds 4–19: Continue to knit two rounds with each colour. Remember to increase in the fifth round [12 sts].
Knit the hoofed hand straight on to each arm in black (see page 20).

The tail:

Transfer the two sets of 5 stitches left on stitch holders on to a set of needles.

Round 1: Join into a round and knit in black [10 sts].

Rounds 2–3: Knit in white.

Rounds 4–5: Knit in black.

Round 6: Using white, k2, k2tog, k2, k2tog, k2 [8 sts].

Rounds 7–11: Knit, maintaining the striped pattern.

Round 12: Using black, k1, k2tog, k2, k2tog, k1 [6 sts].

Round 13: Knit.

Cut off the yarn and pull through the remaining stitches but do not pull tight. Wind black sock yarn a few times around two fingers, wind the yarn around the loops on one side, pull the yarn tight and place in the end of the tail. Now pull the stitches tight and fasten off the yarn (see the photos on pages 56 and 59).

This chart shows half the stitches for Zoe's tail. Continue each round on the second pair of needles, working the chart in mirror image.

Tail chart

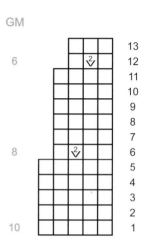

The face:

Knit the forehead (see page 23), then the big nose (page 24), changing colour every two rounds. Begin with white. From round 20 onwards only knit in black.

Embroider the eyes in black on the white stripe at the base of the nose (see page 29).

The left ear:

Pick-up round: Referring to the instructions on pages 27–28, pick up 4 stitches twice on the head for the left ear.

Round 1: Join into a round and knit [8 sts].

Round 2: K1, inc1, k2, inc1, k2, inc1, k2, inc 1, k1 [12 sts].

Round 3: Knit.

Round 4: K3, inc1, k6, inc1, k3 [14 sts].

Rounds 5–8: Knit.

Round 9: K2, k3tog, k4, k3tog, k2 [10 sts].

Round 10: Knit.

Round 11: K2tog, k1, k2tog twice, k1, k2tog [6 sts].

Cut off the yarn, pull through the remaining stitches and finish off.

The right ear:

Pick up stitches for the right ear so that the ears are symmetrical, leaving a gap of about 3 stitches between the ears. Knit the right ear in the same way as the left one.

This chart shows half the stitches for Zoe's ear. Continue each round on the second pair of needles, working the chart in mirror image.

Ear chart

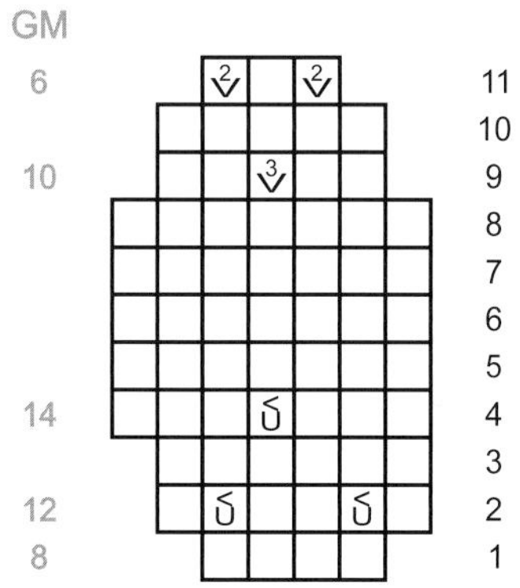

The finishing touches:

For the tuft of hair between the ears, wind black sock yarn a few times around two fingers, wind the yarn around the loops on one side, pull the yarn tight and sew down between the ears.

LARRY LION

Materials

- About 25g (1oz) golden-yellow sock yarn (80% super merino, 20% nylon)
- About 10g (½oz) yellow eyelash yarn for the mane (91% polyamide, 9% polyester)
- Embroidery cotton in black and dark brown
- About 10g (½oz) wadding
- Set of 2.25mm (UK 13/US 1) double-pointed knitting needles

Method

The torso and back of the head:

Using the golden-yellow sock yarn, knit the torso following the instructions on pages 10–12.

Now work the back of the head using the eyelash yarn and following the instructions on page 13 but purl on right-side rows and knit on wrong-side rows (reverse stocking stitch). The hair falls better with the purl stitches.

The lower limbs:

Knit each leg in golden-yellow sock yarn for 20 rounds following the instructions on page 14. Finish with the standard foot (see pages 15–16).

The upper limbs:

Knit each arm in golden-yellow sock yarn for 20 rounds following the instructions on pages 17–18. Finish with a hand with thumb (pages 18–19).

The tail:

Knit the tail in golden-yellow sock yarn as for the zebra (see page 56). Cut off the yarn and pull through the stitches but do not pull tight. Using yellow sewing thread, string together about 10cm (4in) of eyelash yarn so that it can be pulled together in a circle. Put this in the tail and now pull the stitches tight. Finish off tightly.

The face:

Knit the face in golden-yellow sock yarn following the instructions for the cat's face (pages 86–87). Take care on the first two or three rounds not to catch in any of the hair on the back of the head. Embroider the eyes in black and the nose in dark brown embroidery cotton (see page 29).

The ears:

Pick up the stitches for the ears in the mane. Start with the left ear.
Pick-up round: Pick up 7 stitches twice (see page 27).
Round 1: Join into round and knit [14 sts].
Rounds 2–4: Knit.
Round 5: K2tog, k3, k2tog twice, k3, k2tog [10 sts].
Round 6: K2tog, k1, k2tog twice, k1, k2tog [6 sts].
Cut off the yarn, pull through the remaining stitches and finish off. Knit the right ear in the same way.

This chart shows half the stitches for Larry's ear. Repeat the stitches once on each round.

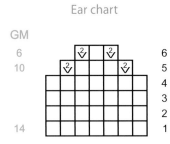

Ear chart

SHELLY SHEEP & PETER WOLF

SHELLY SHEEP

Materials

- About 20g (¾oz) white fluffy sock yarn (39% pure new wool, 61% polyamide) or use an angora mix or similar yarn in a sock weight
- About 10g (½oz) beige sock yarn (80% super marino, 20% nylon)
- Dark brown embroidery thread
- About 10g (½oz) wadding
- Set of 2.5mm (UK 12/US 2) double-pointed knitting needles

Method

The torso and back of the head:

Knit the torso following the instructions on pages 10–12 using white fluffy sock yarn but do not create any stitches for a tail in round 15 or 18.

Directly afterwards, knit the back of the head in the same yarn (see page 13).

The lower limbs:

For the legs and feet use the beige sock yarn. Refer to the instructions below and on pages 14 and 16.

Round 1: Join into a round and knit [12 sts].

Rounds 2–4: Knit.

Round 5: To make the sheep's leg a bit thinner, it should only be increased by 2 stitches. K3, inc1, k6, inc1, k3 [14 sts].

Rounds 6–25: Knit.

Now knit the hoof on to the leg:

Round 1: * Inc1, k1 *, repeat from * to * to the end [28 sts].

Rounds 2–3: Knit.

Round 4: K1, inc1, k12, inc1, k2, inc1, k12, inc1, k1 [32 sts].

Rounds 5–10: Knit.

Round 11: Purl.

Round 12: K2tog to the end [16 sts].

Rounds 13–14: Knit.

Round 15: K2tog to the end [8 sts].

Cut off the yarn, pull through the remaining stitches and finish off.

This chart shows half the stitches for Shelly's foot. Repeat the stitches once on each round.

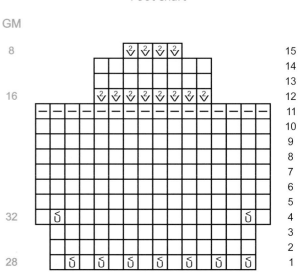

Foot chart

The upper limbs:

For the arms and hands are knitted using the beige sock yarn. To knit each arm, follow the instructions on pages 17–18 but without increasing on round 5. Make each arm 20 rounds long. Finish with the hoofed hand as follows.

Round 1: * K1, inc1 *, repeat from * to * to the end [20 sts].

Rounds 2–6: Knit.

Round 7: Purl.

Round 8: K2tog across the round [10 sts].

Cut off the yarn, pull through the remaining stitches and finish off.

This chart shows half the stitches for Shelly's hoofed hand. Continue each round on the second pair of needles, working the chart in mirror image.

Sheep hand chart

The face:

Lift the stitches left on the stitch holders on to a set of needles. Work in stocking stitch using the beige sock yarn. The face requires short-round shaping.

Start of round: 1st stitch of needle 1.

Round 1: K9, pick up 8 stitches at the side, k17, pick up 8 stitches at the side [9/12/9/12; 42 sts].

Round 2: Follow the instructions for the short-row shaping given for the forehead on page 23 [9/10/9/10; 38 sts].

Rounds 3–4: Begin with the 1st stitch of needle 1. Complete the forehead following the instructions on page 23 [9/9/9/9; 36 sts].

Round 4: Knit.

Round 5: * K1, k2tog, k3, k2tog, k1 *, repeat from * to * three more times [7/7/7/7; 28 sts].

Round 6: Knit.

Stuff the body and the head with wadding.

Round 7 (short-row shaping): K14, leave the stitches of needle 3 for now. Turn work. P21, turn work. K21, knit the 1st stitch of needle 3, turn work. Purl the 1st stitch of needle 3, p21, purl the last stitch of needle 3. Turn work. Knit the last stitch of needle 3 plus the 7 stitches of needle 4.

Rounds 8–13: Continue knitting in rounds.

Stuff the nose with wadding.

Round 14: K2tog fourteen times [14 sts].

Round 15: K2tog seven times [7 sts].

Before pulling together, stuff with some extra wadding, if necessary. Cut off the yarn, pull through the remaining stitches and finish off. Embroider the eyes in dark brown (see page 29).

The left outer ear:

The ears are knitted in two parts with the two different yarns working back and forth in rows of stocking stitch: the outer ear should be worked using the fluffy white yarn and the inner ear with the beige yarn. Start with the left ear.

Pick-up row: Starting at the forehead and using the fluffy white yarn, pick up 5 stitches in a line towards the back of the head.

Row 1: Purl [5 sts].

Row 2: K1, inc1, k3, inc1, k1 [7 sts].

Rows 3–15: Work in stocking stitch.

Row 16: K1, k2tog, k1, k2tog, k1 [5 sts].

Row 17: Purl.

Row 18: Knit.

The left inner ear:

Pick-up row: Using the beige yarn pick up 5 stitches right beside the outer ear.

Row 1: Purl (wrong-side row).

Row 2: Knit.

Rows 3–15: Carry on working in rows of stocking stitch.

Row 16: K2tog, k1, k2tog [3 sts].

Row 17: Purl.

Row 18: K3tog.

Using the beige yarn, sew the inner ear invisibly to the outer ear. As the inner ear is a little shorter and narrower, the ear will curve in a little.

The right ear:

Pick up the stitches for the right outer ear so that the 5th stitch is directly in front on the forehead, parallel with the left ear. Knit the right outer ear and then the inner ear in the same way as for the left ear.

PETER WOLF

Materials

- About 25g (1oz) mid-grey fine alpaca yarn (100% alpaca)
- About 5g (less than ¼oz) light-grey sock yarn (80% super marino, 20% nylon)
- Black embroidery cotton
- About 10g (½oz) wadding
- Set of 2.5mm (UK 12/US 2) double-pointed knitting needles

Method

Most of the wolf should be knitted in mid-grey alpaca but the hands, feet and face should be worked in light-grey sock yarn.

The torso and back of the head:

Knit the torso in the mid-grey alpaca yarn as explained on pages 10–12 from round 1 to round 44 [20 sts].

Round 45: K17. Now slip 9 of the stitches on to stitch holders – the first 2 stitches of needle 4, all 5 stitches from needle 3 and the last 2 stitches of needle 2. Use the remaining 11 stitches for the back of the head: the last 3 stitches of needle 4, all 5 stitches of needle 1 and the first 3 stitches of needle 2.

Row 1 (back of the head): K1, inc1, k1, inc1, k2, * inc1, k1 *, repeat from * to * three more times, k1, inc1, k1, inc1, k1 [19 sts].

Rounds 2–25: Knit following the instructions for the back of the head on page 13.

The lower limbs:

Using the mid-grey alpaca yarn, knit each leg for 20 rounds, following the instructions on page 14, and finish with the standard foot (pages 15–16).

The upper limbs:

Using the mid-grey alpaca yarn, knit each arm for 20 rounds, following the instructions on pages 17–18, and finish with the hand without thumb (page 18).

The tail:

Work in the mid-grey alpaca yarn. Transfer the two sets of 5 stitches left on stitch holders on to a set of needles.

Round 1: Join the stitches into a round and knit [10 sts].

Round 2: Knit.

Round 3: K3, inc1, k4, inc1, k3 [12 sts].

Round 4: Knit.

Round 5: K1, inc1, k4, inc1, k2, inc1, k4, inc1, k1 [16 sts].

Rounds 6–20: Knit.

Stuff the tail with wadding.

Round 21: K2tog, k4, k2tog twice, k4, k2tog [12 sts].

Rounds 22–23: Knit.

Round 24: K2tog, k2, k2tog twice, k2, k2tog [8 sts].

Rounds 25–26: Knit.

Round 27: K2tog four times [4 sts].

Before pulling together, stuff with some extra wadding, if necessary. Cut off the yarn, pull through the remaining stitches and finish off.

This chart shows half the stitches for Peter's tail. Continue each round on the second pair of needles, working the chart in mirror image.

Tail chart

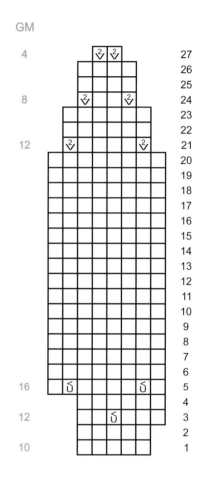

The face:

The wolf's face is knitted in two parts – the upper and lower jaw. These parts are then sewn together.

The upper jaw:

Work in stocking stitch using short-row shaping. The stitches of needle 3 should be set aside to work the lower jaw. Knit on the remaining needles as described here:

Start of row: 1st stitch of needle 4.

Row 1 (pick-up row): Using the light-grey sock yarn, k2, pick up 8 stitches at the side, k9, pick up 8 stitches at the side, k2 [29 sts].

Row 2: Purl.

Row 3: K9, k2tog, k7, k2tog. Turn work (leaving remaining stitches on needles) [27 sts].

Row 4: P8, p2tog, turn work [26 sts].

Row 5: K8, k2tog, turn work [25 sts].

Row 6: P8, p2tog, turn work [24 sts].

Row 7: K8, k2tog, k7 [23 sts].

Row 8: P6, k1, p9, k1, p6.

Row 9: K6, p1, k9, p1, k6.

Row 10: P6, k1, p2tog, p5, p2tog, k1, p6 [21 sts].

Row 11: K6, p1, k7, p1, k6.

Row 12: P6, k1, p7, k1, p6.

Row 13: K1, inc1, k1, inc1, k4, p1, k2tog, k3, k2tog, p1, k4, inc1, k1, inc1, k1 [23 sts].

Row 14: P8, k1, p5, k1, p8.

Row 15: K8, p1, k5, p1, k8.

Row 16: P1, inc1 purlwise, p1, inc1 purlwise, p6, k1, p2tog, p1, p2tog, k1, p6, inc1 purlwise, p1, inc1 purlwise, p1 [25 sts].

Row 17: K10, p1, k3, p1, k10.

Row 18: P10, k1, p3, k1, p10.

Row 19: K2tog, k8, p1, k3, p1, k8, k2tog [23 sts].

Row 20: P2tog, p7, k1, p3, k1, p7, p2tog [21 sts].

Row 21: K2tog, k6, p1, k3, p1, k6, k2tog [19 sts].

Row 22: P2tog, p3, p2tog, k1, p3, k1, p2tog, p3, p2tog [15 sts].

Row 23: K2tog, k1, k2tog, p1, k3, p1, k2tog, k1, k2tog [11 sts].

Row 24: P3tog, k1, p3, k1, p3tog [7 sts].

Row 25: K3tog, k1, k3tog [3 sts].

Cast off the remaining stitches purlwise.

Stuff the body and head with wadding.

This chart shows all the stitches of Peter's upper jaw. The stitches of needle 3 are not used.

Upper jaw chart

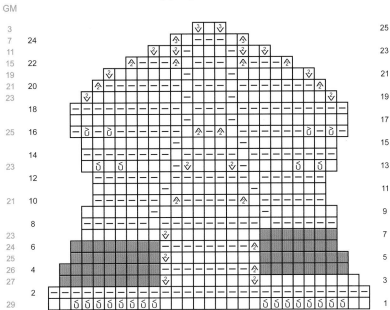

The lower jaw:

For the lower jaw use the 5 stitches left on needle 3.

Use the light-grey sock yarn and work in stocking stitch, knitting right-side rows and purling wrong-side rows.

Start of row: 1st stitch of needle 3.

Row 1: * Inc1, k1 *, repeat from * to * another four times, inc1 [11 sts].

Row 2: Purl.

Rows 3–6: Work in rows of stocking stitch.

Row 7: K1, k2tog, k5, k2tog, k1 [9 sts].

Row 8: Purl.

Row 9: K1, k2tog, k3, k2tog, k1 [7 sts].

Rows 10–15: Work in rows of stocking stitch.

Row 16: P1, p2tog, p1, p2tog, p1 [5 sts].

Row 17: K1, k3tog, k1 [3 sts].

Cast off the remaining stitches purlwise.

Stuff the muzzle with wadding.

Sew the upper and lower jaw together so that the chaps hang down over the top.

This chart shows all the stitches for Peter's lower jaw.

Facial details:

Embroider the eyes and the triangle for the nose in black (see page 29).

The ears:

Start with the left ear.

Pick-up round: Using the mid-grey alpaca yarn, pick up 5 stitches twice on the top of the head for the left ear as explained on pages 27–28.

Round 1: Join into a round and knit [10 sts].

Rounds 2–5: Knit.

Round 6: K2tog, k1, k2tog twice, k1, k2tog [6 sts].

Round 7: Knit.

Round 8: K3tog twice [2 sts].

Cut off the yarn, pull through the remaining stitches and finish off. Make the right ear in the same way, leaving a gap of 2 stitches between the ears.

This chart shows half the stitches for Peter's ear. Repeat the stitches once on each round.

Lower jaw chart

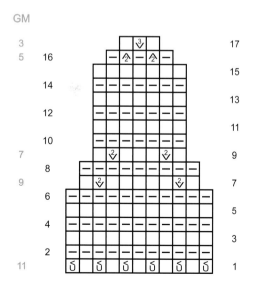

Ear chart

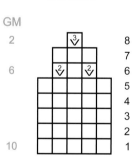

HENRY HORSE & DAISY DONKEY

Horse · About 18cm (7in) high ┊ Donkey · About 19cm (7½in) high

HENRY HORSE

Materials

- About 25g (1oz) chestnut-brown sock yarn (75% wool, 25% nylon)
- About 5g (less than ¼oz) each of sock yarn in mid grey, dark grey and black (80% super merino, 20% nylon)
- About 5g (less than ¼oz) fine yellow alpaca yarn (100% alpaca)
- Black embroidery cotton
- About 10g (½oz) wadding
- Set of 2.25mm (UK 13/US 1) double-pointed knitting needles
- 2.5mm (UK 12, US C/2) crochet hook

Method

The torso and back of the head:

Using the chestnut-brown yarn, knit the torso following the instructions on pages 10–12 and then knit the back of the head (page 13).

The lower limbs:

Using the chestnut-brown yarn, knit each leg for 20 rounds, following the instructions on page 14. Finish with the hoof, following the instructions on page 16 and using the colours below:
Rounds 1–9: Dark grey.
Rounds 10–15: Black.

The upper limbs:

Using the chestnut-brown yarn, knit each arm for 20 rounds, following the instructions on pages 17–18.
Finish with the hoofed hand following the instructions on page 20 and using the colours below:
Rounds 1–5: Dark grey.
Rounds 6–10: Black.

The tail:

Transfer the two sets of 5 stitches left on stitch holders on to a set of needles.

Rounds 1–3: Join the stitches into a round and knit in stocking stitch with the chestnut-brown yarn.

Cut off the yarn and pull through the remaining stitches but do not pull tight. Wind the yellow alpaca yarn about 20 times around three fingers, then wind the yarn tightly around the loops on one side; finish off the yarn and place in the end of the tail. Now pull the stitches tight and finish off. Cut the loops to equal lengths of about 5cm (2in).

The face:

Lift the stitches left on the stitch holders on to a set of needles. Using the chestnut-brown yarn, knit the forehead as instructed on page 23 up to and including round 5 but skipping round 2. Distribution of stitches 9/9/9/9 [36 sts].

The horse has a variation of the large nose.

Round 1: * K1, k2tog, k6 *, repeat from * to * three more times [32 sts].

Rounds 2–11: Knit.

Round 12: Change to mid-grey yarn. * K1, inc1, k6, inc1, k1 *, repeat from * to * three more times [40 sts].

Rounds 13–15: Knit.

Stuff the body and the head with wadding.

Round 16: * K1, k2tog, k4, k2tog, k1 *, repeat from * to * three more times [32 sts].

Round 17: Knit.

Round 18: * K1, k2tog, k2, k2tog, k1 *, repeat from * to * three more times [24 sts].

Round 19: Knit.

Stuff the nose with wadding.

Round 20: * K2tog, k2, k2tog *, repeat from * to * three more times [16 sts].

Cut off the yarn, pull through the remaining stitches and finish off. Embroider the eyes on the face using the black embroidery cotton.

This chart for Henry's nose shows the stitches for the first needle only. Repeat the pattern on each of the four needles.

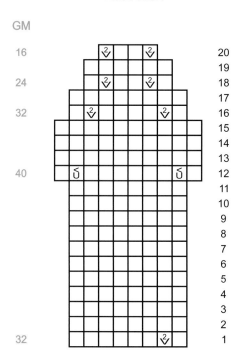

Nose chart

The ears:

Pick-up round: Starting with the left ear, pick up 5 stitches twice following the instructions on pages 27–28.

Round 1: Join into a round and knit [10 sts].

Round 2: Knit.

Round 3: K3, inc1, k4, inc1, k3 [12 sts].

Rounds 4–6: Knit.

Round 7: K2, k2tog, k4, k2tog, k2 [10 sts].

Round 8: Knit.

Round 9: K2tog, k1, k2tog twice, k1, k2tog [6 sts].

Round 10: K3tog twice.

Cut off the yarn, pull through the remaining stitches and finish off. Knit the right ear in the same way, picking up the stitches so that there is a gap of about 3 stitches between the ears.

This chart shows half the stitches for Henry's ear. Continue each round on the second pair of needles, working the chart in mirror image.

The mane:

Cut 20–25 pieces of yellow alpaca yarn, each 20cm (8in) long. Beginning at the centre between the ears, about 3 stitches towards the forehead, work as follows:

Fold a strand of yarn in half. Using the crochet hook, reach under a stitch, hook the two strands of folded yarn in the middle and pull partway through, then pass the yarn ends through the loop formed. Pull tight and trim the four ends to the same length. Repeat this process on the centre stitches of the back of the head until the desired length of mane is reached.

Ear chart

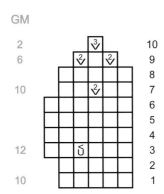

DAISY DONKEY

Materials

- About 25g (1oz) mid-grey sock yarn (80% super merino, 20% nylon)
- About 5g (less than ¼oz) each of sock yarn in dark grey, black and white (80% super merino, 20% nylon)
- About 5g (less than ¼oz) black mohair (70% super kid mohair, 25% polyamide, 5% pure new wool)
- Black embroidery cotton
- About 10g (½oz) wadding
- Set of 2.25mm (UK 13/US 1) double-pointed knitting needles
- 2.5mm (UK 12, US C/2) crochet hook

Method

The torso and back of the head:

Using the mid-grey yarn, knit the torso following the instructions on pages 10–12 and follow with the back of the head (see page 13).

The lower limbs:

Using mid-grey yarn, knit each leg for 20 rounds, following the instructions on page 14. Finish with a hoof, following the instructions on page 16 and using the colours below:

Rounds 1–6: Dark grey.
Rounds 7–15: Black.

The upper limbs:

Using mid-grey yarn, knit each arm for 24 rounds, following the instructions on pages 17–18. Finish with a hoofed hand, following the instructions on page 20 and using the colours below:

Rounds 1–5: Dark grey.
Rounds 6–10: Black.

The tail:

Transfer the two sets of 5 stitches left on stitch holders on to a set of needles.

Rounds 1–5: Using mid-grey yarn, join into a round and knit [10 sts].
Round 6: K2, k2tog, k2, k2tog, k2 [8 sts].
Rounds 7–11: Change to black kid mohair and knit.
Round 12: K1, k2tog, k2, k2tog, k1 [6 sts].
Rounds 13–17: Knit.

Cut off the yarn, pull through the remaining stitches and finish off.

This chart shows half the stitches for Daisy's tail. Continue each round on the second pair of needles, working the chart in mirror image.

Tail chart

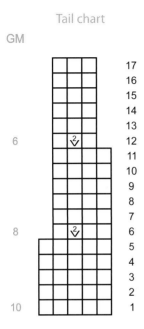

The face:

Lift the stitches left on the stitch holders on to a set of needles. Using mid-grey yarn, knit the forehead following the instructions on page 23 [36 sts].

The nose is a variation of the large nose. Work as follows:

Round 1: Using mid-grey yarn, * k2tog, k7 *, repeat from * to * three more times [32 sts].

Rounds 2–3: Knit.

Round 4: * K6, k2tog *, repeat from * to * three more times [28 sts].

Rounds 5–10: Knit.

Stuff the body and the head with wadding.

Round 11: Change to white yarn. * K2tog, k3, k2tog, k7 *, repeat from * to * once more [24 sts].

Round 12: Knit.

Round 13: * K5, K2tog, k3, k2tog *, repeat from * to * once more [20 sts].

Stuff the nose with wadding.

Rounds 14–18: Knit.

Round 19: * K2tog, k1, k2tog *, repeat from * to * three more times [12 sts].

Before pulling together, stuff with some extra wadding, if necessary. Cut off the yarn, pull through the remaining stitches and finish off. Embroider the eyes using black embroidery cotton (see page 29).

These charts show all the stitches for Daisy's nose. Follow the appropriate chart on each needle.

Nose chart (needles 2 and 4)   Nose chart (needles 1 and 3)

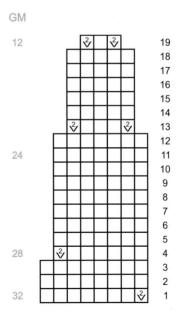
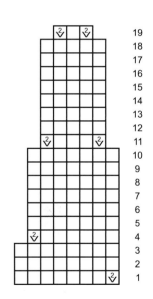

The left outer ear:

The ears are knitted in two parts, in rows of stocking stitch, and then crocheted together with black mohair yarn. Start with the left outer ear and refer to the instructions on pages 27–28.

Pick-up row: Using mid-grey yarn and starting about three rows back from the forehead, pick up 3 stitches on the top of the head and 4 stitches at the side.

Row 1: Purl (wrong-side row) [7 sts].

Row 2: Knit.

Rows 3–17: Work back and forth in rows of stocking stitch.

Row 18: K2tog, k3, k2tog [5 sts].

Row 19: Purl.

Row 20: K2tog, k1, k2tog [3 sts].

Cast off the stitches purlwise.

The left inner ear:

Pick-up row: Using white yarn, pick up 5 stitches directly along the front edge of the outer ear.

Row 1: Purl (wrong-side row) [5 sts].

Row 2: Knit.

Rows 3–15: Work back and forth in rows of stocking stitch.

Row 16: K2tog, k1, k2tog [3 sts].

Rows 17–20: Work back and forth in rows of stocking stitch.

Cast off the stitches purlwise.

Crochet the outer and inner ear together using black kid mohair yarn and using double crochet (US single crochet).

The right ear:

Knit the right ear in the same way as the left one, leaving a gap of about 4 stitches between the ears.

These charts show all the stitches for Daisy's inner and outer ear. Both ears are work the same way.

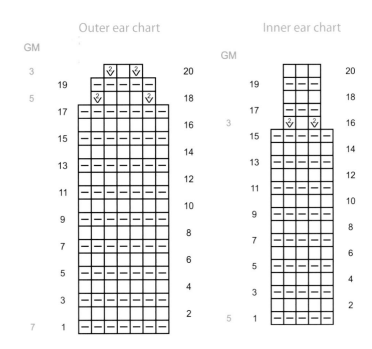

Outer ear chart

Inner ear chart

FeLix Fox & Harry Hare

FeLix Fox

Materials

- About 25g (1oz) sock yarn in chestnut brown and about 5g (less than ¼oz) in black (75% wool, 25% polyamide)
- About 5g (less than ¼oz) each of mohair yarn in black and white (80% super kid mohair, 20% polyamide)
- About 5g (less than ¼oz) russet flecked mohair yarn (80% super kid mohair, 20% polyamide)
- Black embroidery cotton
- About 10g (½oz) wadding
- Sets of double-pointed knitting needles: 2.25mm (UK 13/US 1), 2.5mm (UK 12/US 2), 3mm (UK 11/US 3)
- 2.5mm (UK 12, US C/2) crochet hook

Method

The torso and back of the head:

Using the 2.5mm (UK 12/ US 2) knitting needles and chestnut yarn, knit the torso following the instructions on pages 10–12. Follow with the back of the head (page 13).

The lower limbs:

Using the 2.5mm (UK 12/ US 2) needles, work each leg following the instructions on page 14 and using the colours below:

Rounds 1–15: Chestnut.

Rounds 16–20: Black.

Follow with a standard foot knitted in black yarn (see pages 15–16).

The upper limbs:

Using the 2.5mm (UK 12/ US 2) needles, knit each arm following the instructions on pages 17–18 and using the colours below:

Rounds 1–15: Chestnut.

Rounds 16–20: Black.

Follow with the hand with thumb knitted in black yarn (pages 18–19).

The tail:

Use the 3mm (UK 11/US 3) knitting needles, and one strand of chestnut-brown sock yarn and one strand of russet mohair yarn together. (The tip of the tail is knitted with two strands of white mohair yarn.)

Transfer the two sets of 5 stitches left on stitch holders on to a set of needles.

Round 1: Using one strand of chestnut sock yarn and one strand of russet mohair yarn, join the stitches into a round and knit [10 sts].

Round 2: K2, inc1, k6, inc1, k2 [12 sts].

Round 3: Knit.

Round 4: K1, inc1, k4, inc1, k2, inc1, k4, inc1, k1 [16 sts].

Rounds 5–6: Knit.

Round 7: K1, inc1, k6, inc1, k2, inc1, k6, inc1, k1 [20 sts].

Rounds 8–25: Knit.

Rounds 26–32: Change to two strands of white mohair yarn and knit.

Round 33: K2tog, k16, k2tog [18 sts].

Round 34: Knit.

Round 35: K7, k2tog twice, k7 [16 sts].

Round 36: K2tog, k4, k2tog twice, k4, k2tog [12 sts].

Cut off the yarn and pull through the remaining stitches.

This chart shows half the stitches for Felix's tail. Continue each round on the second pair of needles, working the chart in mirror image.

Tail chart

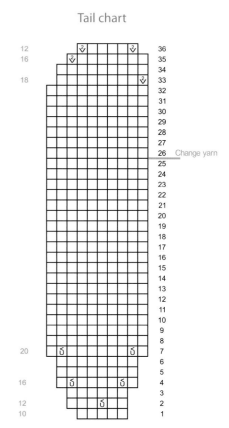

The face:

The face is started with the 2.5mm (UK 12/ US 2) needles and finished with the 2.25mm (UK 13, US 1) needles as follows.

Lift the stitches left on the stitch holders on to a set of needles. Knit the mouse face following the instructions on pages 25–26 and using the colours and needles below:

Rounds 1–8: 2.5mm (UK 12/ US 2) needles and chestnut sock yarn.

Round 9: K14 in chestnut, then change to the 2.25mm (UK 13/ US 1) needles; from here, continue working with two strands of white mohair yarn – work round 9 to the end, following the instructions on page 25.

Rounds 10–20: Finish the face following the instructions on page 25–26.
Embroider the eyes and nose with black embroidery cotton (see page 29).

The left outer ear:
The ears are knitted in two parts in rows of stocking stitch. These are then crocheted together with black mohair yarn. Use the 2.5mm (UK 12/ US 2) needles and start with the left ear.
Pick-up row: Using chestnut sock yarn and referring to the instructions on pages 27–28, pick up 6 stitches for the left ear: 3 stitches on the top of the head and 3 stitches at the side.
Row 1: Purl (wrong-side row) [6 sts].
Row 2: K3, inc1, k3 [7 sts].
Row 3: Purl.
Row 4: Knit.
Row 5: Purl.
Row 6: K2tog, k3, k2tog [5 sts].
Row 7: Purl.
Row 8: K2tog, k1, k2tog [3 sts].
Row 9: Purl.
Row 10: K3tog. Pull the yarn through and fasten off.

The left inner ear:
Use the 2.25mm (UK 13, US 1) knitting needles.
Pick-up row: Using white mohair yarn, pick up 6 stitches directly in front of the outer ear.
Row 1: Purl [6 sts].
Row 2: K3, inc1, k3 [7 sts].
Row 3: Purl.
Row 4: Knit.
Row 5: P2tog, p3, p2tog [5 sts].
Row 6: K2tog, k1, k2tog [3 sts].
Row 7: P3tog. Pull the yarn through.
Crochet the two ear pieces together using two strands of black mohair yarn and double crochet (US single crochet).

The right ear:
Make the right ear in the same way as the left one, leaving a gap of about 4 stitches between the ears and making sure the ears are symmetrical.

The charts for Felix's ears show all the stitches for the left ear. Work the right ear in mirror image.

Outer ear chart   Inner ear chart

HARRY HARE

Materials

- About 25g (1oz) off-white sock yarn (75% wool, 25% polyamide)
- About 5g (less than ¼oz) pink sock yarn (75% wool, 25% polyamide)
- A little fluffy white sock yarn or other fluffy fine yarn for the tail and ear edging (39% pure new wool, 61% polyamide)
- Black embroidery cotton
- About 10g (½oz) wadding
- Set of 2.5mm (UK 12/US 2) double-pointed knitting needles
- 2.5mm (UK 12, US C/2) crochet hook

Method

The torso and back of the head:

Using the off-white yarn, knit the torso following the instructions on pages 10–12. Then work the back of the head (see page 13).

The lower limbs:

Using off-white yarn, knit each leg for 20 rounds following the instructions on page 14. Finish with the standard foot (pages 15–16) in the same colour.

The upper limbs:

Using off-white yarn, knit each arm for 20 rounds following the instructions on pages 17–18. Finish with the hand with thumb (pages 18–19).

The tail:

Use the fluffy sock yarn for the little tail.

Transfer the two sets of 5 stitches left on the stitch holders for the tail on to a set of needles.

Round 1: Knit [10 sts].

Round 2: K3, inc1, k7 [11 sts].

Working extra rows over the first 6 stitches of the next two rounds shapes the tail. Remember to loop the yarn around the next stitch each time before you turn to prevent a hole forming.

Round 3: K6, turn the work and purl back over the 6 stitches, turn the work and knit back over the 6 stitches, k5.

Round 4: K6, turn the work and purl back over the 6 stitches, turn the work and knit back over the 6 stitches, k5.

Rounds 5–8: Knit.

Stuff with some wadding.

Cut off the yarn and pull through the remaining stitches.

Tail chart

GM

11
10

8
7
6
5
4
3
2
1

The chart shows all the stitches for Harry's tail.

The face:

Lift the stitches left on the stitch holders on to a set of needles.

Start of round: 1st stitch of needle 1.

Pick-up round: Using the off-white sock yarn, k9, pick up 8 stitches, k17 (i.e. 4 + 9 + 4 stitches), pick up 8 stitches [9/12/9/12; 42 sts].

Rounds 1–2: Join into a round and knit.

Round 3: K9, k2tog, k8, k2tog twice, k5, k2tog twice, k8, k2tog [9/10/7/10; 36 sts].

Round 4: K2tog, k5, k2tog twice, k3, kfb five times, k2tog, k3, k2tog, kfb five times, k3, k2tog [7/14/5/14; 40 sts].

Round 5: K11, now * k10, turn, p10, turn, k10 *, k5, repeat from * to * once more, k4.

Round 6: K2tog, k3, k2tog twice, k2, * k10, turn, p10, turn, k10 *, k2tog, k1, k2tog, repeat from * to * once more, k2, k2tog [5/13/3/13; 34 sts].

Round 7: Knit all stitches.

Stuff the body and the head with wadding.

Round 8: K2tog, k1, k2tog twice, k25, k2tog [3/12/3/12; 30 sts].

Round 9: Knit all stitches.

Round 10: K5, k2tog five times, k3tog, k2tog five times, k2 [3/7/1/7; 18 sts].

Round 11: K2tog, k1, k2tog, knit to the end [3/6/1/6; 16 sts].

Stuff the muzzle with wadding.

This chart shows all the stitches for Harry's face.

Round 12: K2tog, k1, k2tog twice, k1, k2tog, k1, k2tog, k1, k2tog [3/3/1/3; 10 sts].

Before pulling together, stuff with some extra wadding, if necessary. Cut off the yarn, pull through the remaining stitches and finish off. Embroider the eyes and the triangular nose using black embroidery cotton and following the instructions on page 29.

The left outer ear:

The ears are knitted in two parts, in rows in stocking stitch, and then crocheted together with the white fluffy sock yarn. Knit the left ear first.

Pick-up row: Using off-white sock yarn and referring to the diagram here and the instructions on pages 27–28, pick up 9 stitches for the left ear. Distribute them as three sets of 3 stitches picked up in a curved triangle.

Row 1: Purl (wrong-side row) [9 sts].

Row 2: Knit.

Rows 3–5: Work back and forth in rows of stocking stitch.

Row 6: K3, k3tog, k3 [7 sts].

Rows 7–21: Work back and forth in rows of stocking stitch.

Row 22: K1, k2tog, k1, k2tog, k1 [5 sts].

Row 23: Purl.

Row 24: K2tog, k1, k2tog [3 sts].

Row 25: Purl.

Cast off the remaining stitches knitwise and finish off.

The face chart

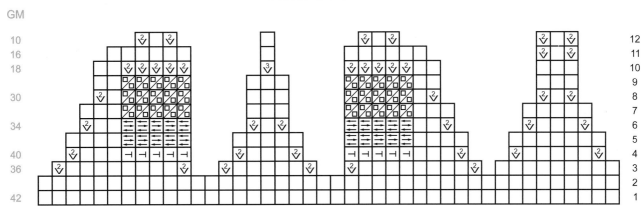

Diagram for picking up stitches for the outer ear

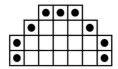

The right ear:

Knit the right ear in the same way as the left one, leaving a gap of about 2 stitches between the ears.

These charts show the stitches for Harry's inner and outer ear.

The left inner ear:

Pick-up round: Using pink sock yarn, pick up 9 stitches directly in front of the outer ear.

Row 1: Purl (wrong-side row) [9 sts].

Row 2: Knit.

Row 3: Purl.

Row 4: K3, k3tog, k3 [7 sts].

Rows 5–11: Work back and forth in rows of stocking stitch.

Row 12: K1, k2tog, k1, k2tog, k1 [5 sts].

Rows 13–19: Work back and forth in rows of stocking stitch.

Row 20: K2tog, k1, k2tog [3 sts].

Rows 21–23: Work back and forth in rows of stocking stitch.

Cast off the remaining stitches knitwise and finish off.

Now crochet together both the ear pieces with fluffy sock yarn using double crochet (US single crochet). As the inner ear is a little shorter, the whole ear will bend forwards.

Outer ear chart   Inner ear chart

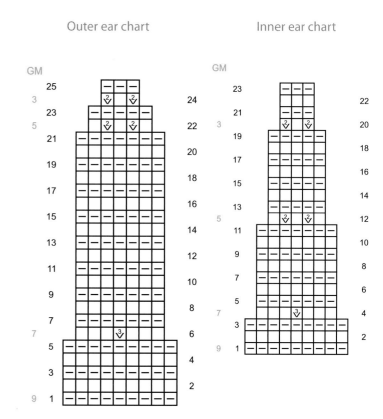

TOMMY TOMCAT & DANNIE DOG

Cat • About 18cm (7in) high | Dog • About 16cm (6¼in) high

TOMMY TOMCAT

Materials

- About 25g (1oz) black sock yarn (80% super merino, 20% nylon)
- About 5g (less than ¼oz) off-white sock yarn (80% super merino, 20% nylon)
- About 3g (less than ¼oz) pale pink mohair yarn (70% super kid mohair, 30% silk)
- Embroidery thread in black, pink and yellow
- About 10g (½oz) wadding
- Set of 2.5mm (UK 12/US 2) double-pointed knitting needles

Method

The torso and back of the head:

Using black yarn, knit the torso following the instructions on pages 10–12. Follow with the back of the head (page 13).

The lower limbs:

Knit each leg for 20 rounds following the instructions on page 14 and using the colours below:

Rounds 1–18: Black.

Rounds 19–20: White.

Finish with the standard foot knitted in white yarn, following the instructions on pages 15–16.

The upper limbs:

Knit each arm for 20 rounds using black yarn and following the instructions on pages 17–18.

Follow with the hand with thumb knitted in white yarn (pages 18–19).

The tail:

Transfer the two sets of 5 stitches set aside for the tail on to a set of needles. Work as follows, stuffing the tail with wadding every 10 rounds:

Rounds 1–2: Join the stitches for the tail into a round and knit using black yarn [10 sts].

Round 3: K3, inc1, k4, inc1, k3 [12 sts].

Rounds 4–5: Knit.

Round 6: * K1, inc1, k4, inc1, k1 *, repeat from * to * once more [16 sts].

Rounds 7–30: Knit.

To achieve a bend in the tail, short rounds are knitted next.

All stitches to be knitted are given.

Round 31: K10, turn work.

Round 32: P12, turn work.

Round 33: K13, turn work.

Round 34: P13, turn work. K2.

Round 35: Starting at the 1st stitch of needle 1, knit the whole round.

Rounds 36–38: Knit.

Round 39: Change to off-white yarn and knit.

Rounds 40–44: Knit.

Round 45: * K2tog, k4, k2tog *, repeat from * to * once more [12 sts].

Round 46: Knit.

Cut off the yarn, pull through the remaining stitches and finish off.

The face:

Lift the stitches left on the stitch holders on to a set of needles (see page 25) [9/4/9/4; 26 sts].

Stitches are increased on the third needle in the pick-up round and 16 new stitches are picked up.

Pick-up round: Using black yarn, K9, pick up 8 stitches, k4, k2, inc1, k2, kfb, k2, inc1, k2, k4, pick up 8 stitches [9/12/12/12; 45 sts].

Round 1: Join into a round and knit.

Round 2: Knit.

Round 3: K2tog, k5, k2tog, * k2tog, k8, k2tog *, repeat from * to * twice more [37 sts].

Rounds 4–6: Knit.

Round 7: K2tog, k3, k2tog, * k2tog, k6, k2tog *, repeat from * to * twice more [29 sts].

Rounds 8–10: Knit.

Stuff the body and head with wadding.

Round 11: K2tog, k1, k2tog, * k2tog, k4, k2tog *, repeat from * to * twice more [21 sts].

Round 12: Knit.

Stuff the nose with wadding.

Round 13: K3, * k2tog three times *, repeat from * to * twice more [12 sts].

Round 14: K6, k3tog, k3 [10 sts].

Before pulling together, stuff with some extra wadding, if necessary. Cut off the yarn, pull through the remaining stitches and finish off.

Embroider the eyes in yellow with the typical cat's perpendicular pupil in black (see page 29).

Embroider the nose and mouth in pink. For the whiskers, pull through two double strands of white embroidery cotton under the nose, loop through and pull tight, cut to a length of about 1.5cm (⅝in).

The left outer ear:

The ears are knitted in two parts, in rows in stocking stitch, and are then sewn together invisibly. Knit the left outer ear first.

Pick-up row: Using black yarn and referring to the instructions on pages 27–28 pick up 9 stitches at the side of the head.

Row 1: Purl (wrong-side row) [9 sts].

Row 2: Knit.

Row 3: Purl.

Row 4: Knit.

Row 5: P2tog, p5, p2tog [7 sts].

Row 6: Knit.

Row 7: P2tog, p3tog, p2tog [3 sts].

Row 8: Knit.

Row 9: P3tog.

Pull the yarn through and finish off.

The left inner ear:

Pick-up row: Pick up 7 stitches with the pink mohair yarn directly in front of the outer ear.

Row 1: Purl [7 sts].

Row 2: Knit.

Row 3: Purl.

Row 4: K2tog, k3, k2tog [5 sts].

Row 5: Purl.

Row 6: Knit.

Row 7: P2tog, p1, p2tog [3 sts].

Row 8: K3tog.

Pull the yarn through. Using the pink yarn, sew the inner ear invisibly to the outer ear.

The right ear:

Knit the right ear in the same way as the left one.

These charts show the stitches for Tommy's inner and outer ears.

Outer ear chart

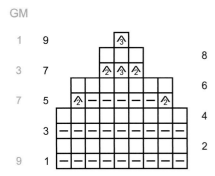

Inner ear chart

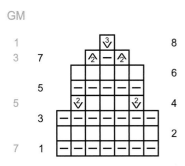

DANNIE THE DOG

Materials

- About 25g (1oz) beige sock yarn (80% super merino, 20% nylon)
- Black embroidery thread
- About 10g (½oz) wadding
- Set of 2.5mm (UK 12/US 2) double-pointed knitting needles

Method

The torso and back of the head:

Rounds 1–44: Knit the torso following the instructions for rounds 1–44 on pages 10–12 [20 sts].

Round 45: K17 then transfer the last 9 knitted stitches you just knitted (first 2 stitches of needle 4, all 5 stitches of needle 3 and the last 2 stitches of needle 2) on to stitch holders.

Use the remaining 11 stitches for the back of the head: the 3 remaining stitches of needle 4, all 5 stitches of needle 1 and the first 3 stitches of needle 2. Work as follows:

Row 1: K1, inc1, k1, inc1, k2, * inc1, k1 *, repeat from * to * another three times, k1, inc1, k1, inc1, k1 [19 sts].

Rounds 2–25: Knit following the instructions for the back of the head on page 13.

The lower limbs:

Knit each leg for 20 rounds following the instructions on page 14 and finish with the standard foot (pages 15–16).

The upper limbs:

Knit each arm for 20 rounds following the instructions on pages 17–18 and finish with the hand without thumb (page 18).

The tail:

Transfer the two sets of 5 stitches set aside for the tail on to a set of needles.

Round 1: Join into a round and knit [10 sts].

Rounds 2–5: Knit.

Round 6: K5, turn work, p5, turn work, k5 (looping the yarn around the next stitch each time before you turn to prevent a hole forming), k2tog, k1, k2tog [8 sts].

Round 7: Knit.

Round 8: K5, turn work, p5, turn work, k5, k3.

Rounds 9–15: Knit.

Stuff the tail with some wadding.

Round 16: K2tog four times [4 sts].

Cut off the yarn, pull through the remaining stitches and finish off.

This chart shows all the stitches for Dannie's tail.

The tail chart

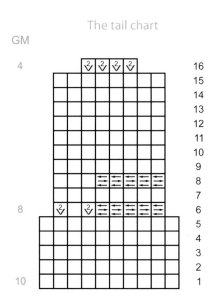

The upper jaw:

The dog's face is knitted in two parts: the upper and lower jaw. These are sewn together afterwards. The upper jaw is knitted first and the stitches of the third needle are left on the stitch holder for the lower jaw.

Work back and forth and in short rows.

Start of row: 1st stitch of needle 4.

Rows 1–14: Work following the instructions for the upper jaw of the wolf on pages 65–66 [23 sts].

Row 15: K1, inc1, k1, inc1, k6, p1, k5, p1, k6, inc1, k1, inc1, k1 [27 sts].

Row 16: P10, k1, p5, k1, p10.

Row 17: K2tog, k8, p1, k5, p1, k8, k2tog [25 sts].

Row 18: P2tog, p7, k1, p5, k1, p7, p2tog [23 sts].

Row 19: K1, k2tog, k3, k2tog, p1, k2tog, k1, k2tog, p1, k2tog, k3, k2tog, k1 [17 sts].

This chart shows the stitches for Dannie's upper jaw, starting at row 15. (The stitches on the third needle should be reserved for the lower jaw.)

Row 20: P1, p2tog, p1, p2tog, k1, p3, k1, p2tog, p1, p2tog, p1 [13 sts].

Row 21: K1, k2tog, k1, p1, k3tog, p1, k1, k2tog, k1 [9 sts].

Cast off the remaining stitches purlwise.

Stuff the body and the head with wadding.

The lower jaw:

Rows 1–11: Work following the instructions for the lower jaw of the wolf on pages 66–67.

Cast off all stitches purlwise.

Stuff the muzzle with wadding.

Sew the lower jaw on to the upper jaw so that the chaps hang down over the top.

The eyes and nose:

Embroider the eyes and the triangular nose in black (see page 29).

Upper jaw chart

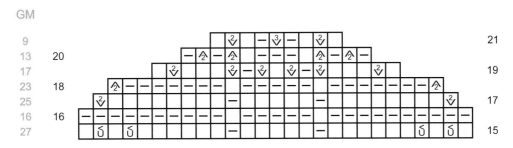

The left ear:

Pick-up round: Pick up 8 stitches twice at a right angle on the head (see pages 27–28).

Round 1: Join into a round and knit [16 sts].

Rounds 2–10: Knit.

Round 11: K2tog, k12, k2tog [14 sts].

Round 12: Knit.

Round 13: K5, k2tog twice, k5 [12 sts].

Round 14: Knit.

Round 15: K2tog six times [6 sts].

Cut off the yarn, pull through the remaining stitches and finish off.

The right ear:

Knit the right ear in the same way as the left one.

This chart shows half the stitches for Dannie's ear. Continue each round on the second pair of needles, working the chart in mirror image.

Ear chart

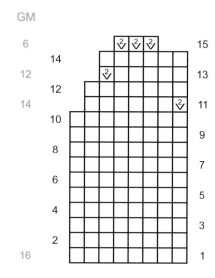

90

BENJAMIN BEAR & PATRICIA PANDA

Bear · About 19cm (7½in) high | Panda bear · About 17cm (6¾in) high

BENJAMIN BEAR

Materials

- About 30g (1oz) fine dark-brown alpaca yarn (100% alpaca)
- About 2g (a remnant) fine mid-brown mohair yarn
  (20% kid mohair, 57% merino, 23% polyamide)
- Embroidery cotton in black and mid brown
- About 10g (½oz) wadding
- Set of 2.5mm (UK 12/US 2) double-pointed knitting needles

Method

The torso and back of the head:
Using dark-brown alpaca yarn, knit the torso following the instructions on pages 10–12 and follow with the back of the head (page 13).

The lower limbs:
Using dark-brown alpaca yarn, knit each leg for 15 rounds following the instructions on page 14. Finish with the standard foot (pages 15–16).

The upper limbs:
Using dark-brown alpaca yarn, knit each arm for 15 rounds following the instructions on pages 17–18. Finish with the hand without thumb (page 18).

The little tail:
Round 1: Using dark-brown yarn, join the tail stitches into a round and knit [10 sts].
Rounds 2–4: Knit.
Round 5: K2tog, k1, k2tog twice, k1, k2tog [6 sts].
Do not stuff the tail with wadding.
Cut off the yarn and pull through the remaining stitches.

The face:

Lift the stitches left on the stitch holders on to a set of needles. All stitches to be knitted are given.

Pick-up round: Using dark-brown yarn, k9, pick up 8 stitches at the side, knit 4 + 9 + 4 stitches, pick up 8 stitches at the side [9/12/9/12; 42 sts].

Round 1: Join into round and knit.

Rounds 2–7: Knit.

Round 8: Knit as for round 3 of the forehead (see page 23) [9/10/9/10; 38 sts].

Round 9: Knit as for round 4 of the forehead [9/9/9/9; 36 sts].

Round 10: Knit.

Round 11: * K1, k2tog, k3, k2tog, k1 *, repeat from * to * three more times [28 sts].

Round 12: Knit.

Stuff the body and the head with wadding.

Round 13: This comprises several short rows but for reference purposes we will call this all round 13. K14, leaving the stitches of the third needle. Turn work. P21, turn work. K21, knit the 1st stitch of needle 3, turn work. P22, purl the last stitch of needle 3, turn work. Knit the last stitch of needle 3 and 7 stitches of needle 4.

Rounds 14–15: Knit full rounds.

Stuff the nose with wadding.

Round 16: K2tog fourteen times [14 sts].

Before pulling together, stuff with some extra wadding, if necessary. Cut off the yarn, pull through the remaining stitches and finish off. Embroider the eyes using black embroidery cotton then embroider the nose and mouth in mid brown (see page 29).

The left outer ear:

The ears are knitted in two parts, in rows of stocking stitch, and then invisibly sewn together. Start with the left ear.

Pick-up row: Using dark-brown alpaca yarn and referring to the instructions on pages 27–28, pick up 3 stitches on the top of the head and 4 stitches at the side.

Row 1: Purl (wrong-side row) [7 sts].

Row 2: Knit.

Rows 3–5: Work in row of stocking stitch.

Row 6: K1, k2tog, k1, k2tog, k1 [5 sts].

Cast off the stitches purlwise.

The left inner ear:

Pick-up row: Using mid-brown mohair yarn, pick up 6 stitches directly in front of the outer ear.

Row 1: Purl (wrong-side row) [6 sts].

Row 2: Knit.

Row 3: Purl.

Row 4: Knit.

Row 5: P1, p2tog twice, p1 [4 sts].

Cast off the stitches knitwise.

Sew the inner ear invisibly on to the outer ear using the mid-brown yarn and finish off the yarn ends.

The right ear:

Work the right ear in the same way as the left one, leaving a gap of about 5 stitches between the ears.

These charts show all the stitches for Benjamin's outer and inner ears.

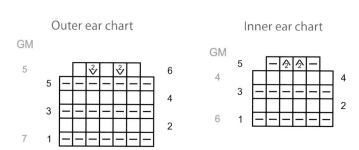

Outer ear chart   Inner ear chart

PATRICIA PANDA

Materials

- About 15g (½oz) each soft kid mohair yarn in white and black (70% super kid mohair, 25% polyamide, 55 pure new wool)
- Black embroidery cotton
- About 10g (½oz) wadding
- Set of 2.5mm (UK 12/US 2) double-pointed knitting needles

Method

The torso:

Rounds 1–28: Using white yarn, knit the torso following the instructions on pages 10–11 for rounds 1–28.

Rounds 29–41: Change to black yarn and continue to follow the instructions (rounds 29–41).

Round 42: Change to white and knit.

Rounds 43–44: Knit [7/7/7/7; 28 sts].

From here, the head starts.

Round 45: Knit 7 + 7 + 7 + 3 stitches. Now slip the last 13 stitches that you have just knitted on to stitch holders. You will begin the back of the head with the 4th stitch of needle 4 (the first of the 4 stitches left on needle 4).

The back of the head:

Start of row: 4th stitch of needle 4, working over the 15 stitches still on the needles:

Row 1: K3, inc1, k2, inc1, k5, inc1, k2, inc1, k3 [19 sts].

Remaining rows: Follow the instructions for knitting the back of the head starting at row 4 (see page 13).

The lower limbs:

Knit each leg in black for 12 rounds following the instructions on page 14 and finish with the standard foot (pages 15–16).

The upper limbs:

Knit each arm in black, following the instructions below and referring to pages 17–18.

Rounds 1–4: Knit.

Round 5: * K1, inc1, k3, inc1, k1 *, repeat from * to * once more [14 sts].

Rounds 6–15: Knit.

Increasing for the hand without thumb:

Round 1: * K1, inc1, k1, inc1, k3, inc1, k1, inc1, k1 *, repeat from * to * once more [22 sts].

Rounds 2–9: Continue working as for the pattern for the hand without thumb (see page 18).

The little tail:

Knit the tail in white following the instructions for the bear (see page 92).

The face:

Use the stitches left on the stitch holders – 9/2/9/2 [22 sts].

Lift the stitches from the stitch holders on to a set of needles.

Work in short rounds of stocking stitch as follows:

Round 1 (pick-up round): K9, pick up 9 stitches, k1, inc1, k1, k9, k1, inc1, k1, pick up 9 stitches [9/12/9/12; 42 sts].

Round 2: K21, turn work.

Round 3: P30, turn work.

Round 4: K 31, turn work.

Round 5: P32, turn work, k13.

Round 6: K21, k2tog, k5, k2tog, k12 [40 sts].

Round 7: K19, k2tog, turn work.

Round 8: P30, p2tog, turn work, k11 [9/11/7/11; 38 sts].

Stuff the body and head with wadding.

For the characteristic black patches around the eyes, cut off two 80cm (31½in) lengths of black mohair yarn and use one for each area around the eye. Refer to the chart to see which stitches should be worked in black. These stitches are tinted green in the chart.

Round 9: This 'round' to create the characteristic eye patches incorporates a series of short rows but for reference purposes it will all be called round 9.

Row 1: Knit together the last stitch of needle 4 with the 1st stitch of needle 1, k7, k2tog, turn work.

Row 2: P8, p2tog, turn work.

Row 3: K8, k2tog, turn work.

Row 4: P8, p2tog, turn work.

Row 5: K8, k2tog, turn work.

Rows 6–8: Repeat rows 4 and 5.

Row 9: K8, k2tog, join into the round again, knit 6 + 7 + 6 stitches.

Round 10: K9, k6, k2tog, k3, k2tog, k6 [9/6/5/6; 26 sts].

Round 11: K2tog, k5, k2tog, k17 [7/6/5/6; 24 sts].

Rounds 12–18: Knit.

Stuff the nose with wadding.

Round 19: K2tog, k3, k2tog, k4, k2tog, k5, k2tog, k4 [5/5/5/5; 20 sts].

Cut off the yarn and pull through the remaining stitches.

Embroider the eyes on the black eye patches using black embroidery thread (see page 29) and then embroider the nose.

This chart shows the stitches for working Patricia's eye patches. The stitches that should be worked with black yarn are tinted green.

Eye patches chart ('round' 9)

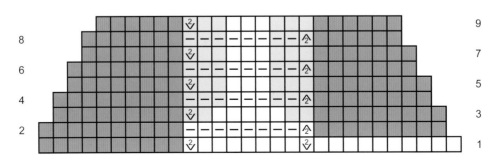

The ears:

Start with the left ear.

Pick-up round: Using black yarn, and referring to the instructions on pages 27–28, pick up 7 stitches twice – 4 stitches on the top of the head and 3 stitches at the side.

Round 1: Join into round and knit [14 sts].

Rounds 2–4: Knit.

Round 5: K2tog, k3, k2tog twice, k3, k2tog [10 sts].

Round 6: K2tog, k1, k2tog twice, k1, k2tog [6 sts].

Cast off the remaining stitches together.

Work the right ear in the same way, leaving a gap of about 3 stitches between the ears.

This chart shows half the stitches for Patricia's ear. Repeat the stitches once on each round.

Ear chart

97

UNI THE UNICORN
& DONALD THE DRAGON

Unicorn • About 25cm (10in) high | Dragon • About 23cm (9in) high

UNI THE UNICORN

Materials

- About 40g (1½oz) white fluffy sock yarn (39% pure new wool, 61% polyamide)
- About 10g (½oz) silver-grey cotton yarn (60% cotton, 40% viscose)
- About 4g (less than ¼oz) pink mohair yarn (70% super kid mohair, 30% silk)
- Black embroidery cotton
- About 20g (¾oz) wadding
- Set of 2.5mm (UK 12/US 2) double-pointed knitting needles
- Set of 3.0mm (UK 11/US 3) double-pointed knitting needles

The modular approach, which is at the heart of this book, is easily transferred to thicker yarns. Here are two magical friends as an example of this.

Method

The torso and back of the head:

Rounds 1–32: Using white fluffy sock yarn, and the 3.0mm (UK 11/US 3) knitting needles, knit the torso following the instructions on pages 10–11 up to and including round 32. Rounds 33 onwards: Work an extra three rounds before continuing the torso from round 33 following the instructions on pages 11–12. Knit the back of the head straight on to the body (page 13).

The lower limbs:

Using the 3.0mm (UK 11/US 3) knitting needles, knit each leg in white fluffy yarn for 25 rounds following the instructions on page 14. Finish by knitting the hoof in silver-grey cotton yarn (see page 16).

The upper limbs:

Using the 3.0mm (UK 11/US 3) knitting needles, knit each arm in white fluffy yarn for 23 rounds following the instructions on pages 17–18. Finish with the hoofed hand worked in silver-grey cotton yarn (page 20).

The tail:

Rounds 1–3: Knit the tail with white fluffy sock yarn following the instructions for the horse's tail (see page 70). Add a tassel to the end of the tail in silver-grey cotton yarn in the same way as for the horse's tail. Trim the yarn to about 8cm (3¼in) or the length desired (see the photo on page 109).

The face:

Using the 3.0mm (UK 11/US 3) knitting needles, follow the instructions for working the horse's face (see page 17) but using the colours below:

Rounds 1–11: White.

Rounds 12–25: Silver grey.

Embroider the eyes using black embroidery cotton (see page 29).

The left outer ear:

The ears are knitted in two parts, working in rows of stocking stitch. These are then sewn together. Start with the left ear.

Pick-up round: Using the white fluffy yarn, and referring to the instructions on pages 27–28, pick up 5 stitches with the 2.5mm (UK 12/ US 2) needles: 3 stitches on the top of the head and 2 stitches at the side.

Row 1: Purl (wrong-side row) [5 sts].

Row 2: Knit.

Row 3: P2, inc1 purlwise, p3 [6 sts].

Rows 4–7: Work back and forth in rows of stocking stitch.

Row 8: K2, k2tog, k2 [5 sts].

Row 9: P2tog, p1, p2tog [3 sts].

Row 10: K3tog.

Pull the yarn through and finish off.

The left inner ear:

Pick-up row: Using two strands of the pink mohair yarn and the 2.5mm (UK 12/ US 2) needles, pick up 5 stitches directly in front of the outer ear.

Row 1: Purl (wrong-side row) [5 sts].

Row 2: Knit.

Rows 3–5: Work back and forth in rows of stocking stitch.

Row 6: K1, k3tog, k1 [3 sts].

Row 7: Purl.

Row 8: K3tog [1 st]. Pull the yarn through.

Using the pink mohair yarn, sew the inner ear invisibly on to the outer ear.

The right ear:

Knit the right ear in the same way as the left one, leaving a gap of about 4 stitches between the ears.

These charts show all the stitches for Uni's left inner and outer ear. Make sure the ears are symmetrical.

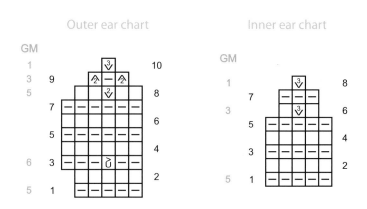

Outer ear chart   Inner ear chart

The mane:

Work the mane in silver-grey cotton yarn following the instructions for the horse's mane (see page 71). Trim the mane to about 3cm (1¼in) long.

The horn:

Using the silver-grey yarn and the larger needles, pick up 2 stitches four times in the centre of the forehead in the form of a square.

Round 1: Join into round and knit [8 sts].

Rounds 2–7: Knit.

Round 8: K2, k2tog, k2, k2tog [6 sts].

Cut off the yarn and pull through the remaining stitches.

Do not stuff the horn with wadding.

DONALD THE DRAGON

Materials

- About 35g (1¼oz) variegated green/blue sock yarn (75% wool, 25% polyamide)
- About 10g (½oz) light-green sock yarn (75% wool, 25% polyamide)
- About 10g (½oz) fine gold Lurex crochet yarn
  (65% viscose, 35% metallic polyester)
- Black embroidery cotton
- About 15g (½oz) wadding
- Set of 2.5mm (UK 12/US 2) double-pointed knitting needles
- Set of 3.0mm (UK 11/US 3) double-pointed knitting needles
- 2.5mm (UK 12 US C/2) crochet hook

Method

Donald is knitted with one strand of the variegated or light-green sock yarn and one strand of fine gold crochet yarn, except for the inside of the wings and the inner ears, which are knitted with one strand of light-green sock yarn.

The torso and back of the head:

Use the 3.0mm (UK 11/US 3) knitting needles.

Rounds 1–32: Using one strand of variegated yarn and one strand of gold crochet yarn together, knit the torso following the instructions on pages 10–11 for rounds 1–32, but only create the stitches for the tail in round 15, not in round 18.

Rounds 33 onwards: Knit an extra three rounds and then continue working from round 33 following the instructions on pages 11–12. Now knit the back of the head straight on to the body (page 13).

The lower limbs:

Using one strand of variegated yarn and one strand of gold crochet yarn together, knit each leg for 20 rounds following the instructions on page 14. Finish with the standard foot (pages 15–16). Use the 3.0mm (UK 11/US 3) knitting needles.

The upper limbs:

Using one strand of variegated yarn and one strand of gold crochet yarn together, knit each arm for 20 rounds following the instructions on pages 17–18. Finish with the four-fingered hand (pages 19–20). Use the 3.0mm (UK 11/US 3) knitting needles.

Square stitches were reserved when knitting the torso. Round stitches should be picked up for the dragon's tail.

Tail pick-up chart

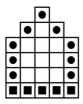

The tail:

For the tail, the stitches are picked up in such a way that the end has a triangular cross section. Use the 3.0mm (UK 11/US 3) knitting needles.

Pick-up round: Using one strand of variegated yarn and one strand of gold crochet yarn together, lift the 5 stitches set aside for the tail when making the torso and knit. Then pick up 9 stitches as shown in the chart.

Round 1: Join into round and knit [14 sts].

Rounds 2–15: Knit.

Round 16: K5, k2tog, k5, k2tog [12 sts].

Rounds 17–25: Knit.

Round 26: K5, k2tog, k3, k2tog [10 sts].

Rounds 27–35: Knit.

Round 36: Change to one strand of light-green sock yarn and one strand of gold crochet yarn; knit all stitches.

Round 37: * Kfb twice, k1, kfb twice *, repeat from * to * once more [18 sts].

Rounds 38–39: Knit.

Round 40: K2tog, k5, k2tog twice, k5, k2tog [14 sts].

Round 41: K2tog, k3, k2tog twice, k3, k2tog [10 sts].

Round 42: K2tog, k1, k2tog twice, k1, k2tog [6 sts].

Round 43: K3tog twice [2 sts].

Cast off the last 2 stitches.

The tail is not stuffed with wadding, but you can stuff it if preferred.

The face and lower lip:

Lift the stitches left on the stitch holders on to a set of needles. Use the 3.0mm (UK 11/US 3) knitting needles.

Rounds 1–15: Knit following the instructions for the monkey's face (see pages 36–37) using the following colours:

Rounds 1–4: One strand of flecked sock yarn and one strand of gold crochet yarn.

Round 5: Knit 29 stitches and then change to one strand of light-green sock yarn and one strand of gold crochet yarn to knit the last 3 stitches. Knit to the end of the nose with these yarns. Distribution of stitches after round 15: 13/1/13/1 [28 sts].

Stuff the body and the head with wadding.

Round 16: K14, k2tog, k3, k3tog, k3, k2tog, k1 [13/1/9/1; 24 sts].

Round 17: K13, k2tog, k7, k2tog [13/0/9/0; 22 sts].

Redistribute the stitches over two needles: 13 stitches on needle 1 and 9 stitches on needle 2.

Round 18 (includes short-row shaping):

Needle 1: K13.

Needle 2: K2tog, k1, k3tog, k1, k2tog [13/5; 18 sts]. Turn the work.

Row 2: P5, slip 1 stitch, p1, pass 1st stitch over, p2tog. Turn work.

Row 3: Slip 1 stitch, k2tog, pass 1st stitch over. Cut off the yarn, pull through and finish off. This is the lower lip. Stuff the nose with wadding.

The upper lip:

There are still 13 stitches on needle 1. Redistribute these over three needles: 5/3/5 [13 sts]. You will be working in short rows of stocking stitch. Only the stitches to be knitted are given.

Start of row: 1st stitch of needle 3.

Row 1: K2, k2tog [12 sts but you have only 3 worked stitches on the left needle]. Turn work.

Row 2: P2, p2tog, turn work [11 sts].

Row 3: K2, k2tog, turn work [10 sts].

Row 4: P2, p2tog, turn work [9 sts].

Row 5: K2, k2tog, turn work [8 sts].

Row 6: P2, p2tog, turn work [7 sts].

Row 7: K2, k2tog, turn work [6 sts].

Row 8: P2, p2tog, turn work [5 sts].

Row 9: K4.

Row 10: P5.

Row 11: K5.

Row 12: P5.

Cast off all 5 stitches knitwise.

Before pulling together, stuff with some extra wadding, if necessary. Put the upper lip inside the lower lip so that the lower lip sticks out and then sew together invisibly.

This chart shows all the stitches for Donald's upper lip. The first round begins at RB.

Upper lip chart

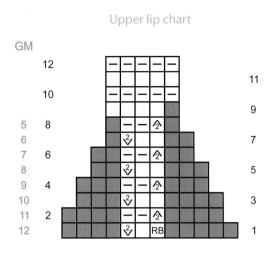

The eyes:

Embroider the eyes with black embroidery cotton (see page 29).

The horns:

The two horns sit right on top of the head and are not stuffed with wadding. Use the 3.0mm (UK 11/US 3) knitting needles.

Horn pick-up chart

Pick up the stitches for each horn as shown in this chart. Place the horns symmetrically on Donald's head.

Pick-up round: Using one strand of light-green sock yarn and one strand of gold crochet yarn, pick up the stitches for each horn on the top of the dragon's head in the square formation shown in the diagram.

Round 1: Join the stitches into a round and knit [12 sts].

Rounds 2–3: Knit.

Round 4: * K1, k2tog twice, k1 *, repeat from * to * once more [8 sts].

Rounds 5–6: Knit.

Round 7: K2tog four times [4 sts].

Cut off the yarn, pull through the remaining stitches and fasten off.

Horn chart

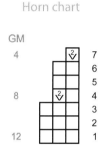

This chart shows a quarter of the stitches for Donald's horn. Repeat the chart in mirror image for the stitches of the second needle and then work the whole thing again over the third and fourth needles.

The left outer ear:

The ears are knitted in two parts, working back and forth in rows of stocking stitch, and are then invisibly sewn together. Begin with the left ear and use the 3.0mm (UK 11/US 3) knitting needles.

Pick-up round: Using one strand of variegated yarn and one strand of fine gold crochet yarn together, pick up 5 stitches at a right angle at the side of the head (see pages 27–28).

Row 1: Purl [5 sts].

Row 2: K1, inc1, k3, inc1, k1 [7 sts].

Rows 3– 5: Work back and forth in rows of stocking stitch.

Row 6: K2tog, k3, k2tog [5 sts].

Rows 7–9: Work in rows of stocking stitch.

Row 10: K2tog, k1, k2tog [3 sts].

Rows 11–12: Work in rows of stocking stitch.

Row 13: P3tog.

The left inner ear:

Using one strand of light-green sock yarn pick up 5 stitches directly in front of the outer ear. Knit the inner ear following the instructions for the outer ear. Sew the inner ear to the outer ear using the light-green yarn.

The right ear:

Work the right ear in the same way as the left one.

The chart opposite shows all the stitches for Donald's ear. The inner and outer ears use the same pattern.

The wings:

The wings are knitted in two parts, in rows of stocking stitch that are then crocheted together with two lengths of gold crochet yarn. The outer wing should be knitted with one strand of variegated yarn and one strand of fine gold crochet yarn using the 3.0mm (UK 11/US 3) needles. The inner wings should be knitted with only one strand of light-green sock yarn and the 2.5mm (UK 12/ US 2) needles.

Ear chart

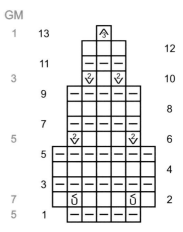

The left outer wing:

Row 1 (pick-up row): Using one strand of variegated yarn and one strand of gold crochet yarn together, pick up and knit 9 stitches on the back, on the left, next to the centre stitch, working from the shoulder in the direction of the tail.

Row 2: Purl [9 sts].

Row 3: K1, inc1, k4, inc1, k4 [11 sts].

Row 4: Purl.

Row 5: K1, inc1, k5, inc1, k5 [13 sts].

Row 6: Purl.

Row 7: K1, inc1, k6, inc1, k6 [15 sts].

Row 8: Purl.

Row 9: K1, inc1, k7, inc1, k7 [17 sts].

Row 10: Purl.

Row 11: K1, inc1, k8, inc1, k8 [19 sts].

Row 12: Purl.

Row 13: K1, inc1, k9, inc1, k9 [21 sts].

Row 14: Purl.

Row 15: K1, inc1, k10, inc1, k10 [23 sts].

Row 16: Purl all stitches.

From here, the two tips of the wings are knitted individually to the end. Knit in short rows. Only the stitches to be knitted are given.

First left wing tip:

Row 17: Cast off 2 stitches, k4, turn work.

Row 18: P4, turn work.

Row 19: K6, turn work.

Row 20: P6, turn work.

Row 21: K8, turn work.

Row 22: P8, turn work.

Cast off 11 stitches knitwise (10 stitches remain on the needle).

Second left wing tip:

Row 17: K4, turn work.

Row 18: P4, turn work.

Row 19: K6, turn work.

Row 20: P6, turn work.

Row 21: K8, turn work.

Row 22: P8, turn work.

Cast off 10 stitches knitwise, casting off the last 2 stitches together.

This chart shows the pattern for Donald's left outer wing.

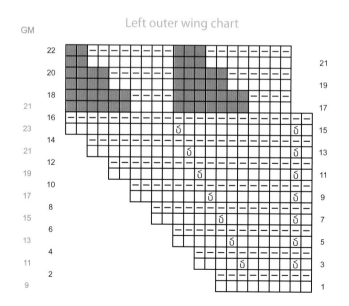

Left outer wing chart

The right outer wing:

Row 1 (pick-up row): Using one strand of variegated yarn and one strand of gold crochet yarn together, pick up and knit 9 stitches on the back, on the right, next to the centre stitch, at the same height as the left wing, starting at the tail and working in the direction of the shoulder.

Row 2: Purl all stitches [9 sts].

Row 3: K4, inc1, k4, inc1, k1 [11 sts].

Row 4: Purl.

Row 5: K5, inc1, k5, inc1, k1 [13 sts].

Row 6: Purl.

Row 7: K6, inc1, k6, inc1, k1 [15 sts].

Row 8: Purl.

Row 9: K7, inc1, k7, inc1, k1 [17 sts].

Row 10: Purl.

Row 11: K8, inc1, k8, inc1, k1 [19 sts.]

Row 12: Purl.

Row 13: K9, inc1, k9, inc1, k1 [21 sts].

Row 14: Purl.

Row 15: K10, inc1, k10, inc1, k1 [23 sts].

Row 16: Purl.

Row 17: Knit.

From here, the two tips of the wings are knitted individually to the end. Knit in short rows. Only the stitches to be knitted are given.

First outer right wing:

First outer right wing tip:

Row 18: Cast off 2 stitches purlwise, p4. Turn work.

Row 19: K4, turn work.

Row 20: P6, turn work.

Row 21: K6, turn work.

Row 22: P8, turn work.

Row 23: K8, turn work.

Cast off 11 stitches purlwise (10 stitches remain on the needle).

Second outer right wing tip:

Row 18: P4, turn work.

Row 19: K4, turn work.

Row 20: P6, turn work.

Row 21: K6, turn work.

Row 22: P8, turn work.

Row 23: K8, turn work.

Cast off 10 stitches purlwise, casting off the last 2 stitches together.

First inner left wing tip:

Row 18: Cast off 2 stitches purlwise. P5, turn work.

Row 19: K5, turn work.

Row 20: P7, turn work.

Row 21: K7, turn work.

Row 22: P9, turn work.

Row 23: K9, turn work.

Cast off 12 stitches purlwise (11 stitches remain on the needle).

The left inner wing:

Row 1 (pick-up row): Using only one strand of light-green sock yarn and the 2.5mm (UK 12/ US 2) needles, pick up and knit 9 stitches directly along the outside of the left outer wing, starting at the tail and working in the direction of the shoulder.

Rows 2–16: Knit following the instructions for the right outer wing.

Row 17: K11, inc1, k11, inc1, k1 [25 sts].

This chart shows the pattern for Donald's right outer wing.

Second inner left wing tip:

Row 18: P5, turn work.

Row 19: K5, turn work.

Row 20: P7, turn work.

Row 21: K7, turn work.

Row 22: P9, turn work.

Row 23: K9, turn work.

Cast off 12 stitches purlwise, casting off the last 2 stitches together.

Right outer wing chart

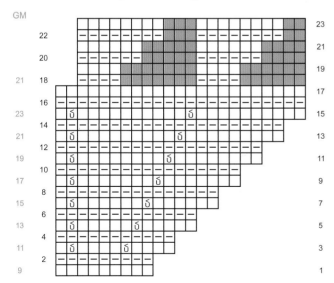

This chart shows the pattern for Donald's left inner wing from row 17.

Left inner wing chart

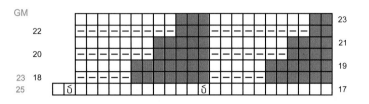

This chart shows the pattern for Donald's right inner wing from row 17.

Right inner wing chart

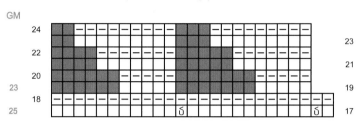

The inner right wing:

Row 1 (pick-up row): Using only one strand of light-green sock yarn and the 2.5mm (UK 12/ US 2) needles, pick up 9 stitches directly along the outside of the right outer wing, starting at the head and working in the direction of the tail.

Rows 2–16: Knit following the instructions for the left outer wing.

Row 17: K1, inc1, k11, inc1, k11 [25 sts].

Row 18: Purl.

First inner right wing tip:

Row 19: K5, turn work.

Row 20: P5, turn work.

Row 21: K7, turn work.

Row 22: P7, turn work.

Row 23: K9, turn work.

Row 24: P9, turn work.

Cast off 12 stitches knitwise (11 stitches remain on the needle).

Second inner right wing tip:

Row 19: K5, turn work.

Row 20: P5, turn work.

Row 21: K7, turn work.

Row 22: P7, turn work.

Row 23: K9, turn work.

Row 24: P9, turn work.

Cast off 11 stitches knitwise, casting off the last 2 stitches together.

Finishing the wings:

Crochet together the inner and outer wings using two strands of gold yarn and working in double crochet (US single crochet).